THE HOW-TO BOOK OF
FLOORS & CEILINGS

THE HOW-TO BOOK OF FLOORS & CEILINGS

By Don Geary

TAB BOOKS

BLUE RIDGE SUMMIT, PA. 17214

FIRST EDITION

FIRST PRINTING—JULY 1978

Copyright © 1978 by TAB BOOKS

Printed in the United States
of America

Library of Congress Cataloging in Publication Data

Geary, Don.
    The how-to-book of floors & ceilings.

"TAB #998."
    Includes index.
    1. Floors—Amateurs' manuals. 2. Ceilings—Amateurs' man-
uals I. Title.   TH2521.G4   698.9   77-18952
ISBN 0-8306-8998-2
ISBN 0-8306-7998-7 pbk.

Cover photos by the makers of Armstong interior furnishings.

Preface

Home remodeling is no longer the exclusive realm of the professional. Do-it-yourselfers found out years ago that they could usually match professional workmanship—maybe even go it one better. And you can, too. Sweat, determination, information—that's all it takes to remodel a room, to give it a whole new look. And that's what this book is all about—breaking out of the mold, tearing away the old flooring and ceiling and applying coverings that suit your fancy—and your pocketbook.

This book gives you step-by-step instructions on how to lay new subflooring, nonceramic tile, sheet vinyl, wood flooring, and ceramic tile. The directions are clear and easy to follow, written for the first-time remodeler. There are detailed tools and materials lists—and lots of commonsense tips on planning your new flooring, from selection of colors to deciding where every piece of flooring will go.

And that's only half the good news: the art of installing new ceilings is no longer a trade secret; this volume gives you a complete course in everything from putting up wooden box beams to hanging a suspended ceiling to installing a skylight.

Of course, in writing this book, I received a lot of help from my friends. I would like to thank the following companies for supplying me with valuable information:

Acoustical Materials Association
American Albino Association

American Plywood Association
Azrock
Black & Decker
Flintkote
Georgia-Pacific
National Association of Home Workshop Writers
Scovill Lighting
U.S. Gypsum
Weyerhaeuser Company
American Olean
Armstrong Cork Company
Barclay Industries
California Redwood Association
GAF Corporation
Monaco Brothers
Wasco Skywindows

Don Geary

Contents

Chapter 1
The Anatomy
of House Floors

In an effort to make the first half of this book more meaningful and useful, I have decided to make this opening chapter a kind of explanation—a primer, if you will—of how floors are commonly constructed. Carpentry, remodeling, and home repairs will be much easier to accomplish if we have a basic understanding of how things are done by professional builders. There are, after all, no secrets to building a house. In fact, building a house is a project that can be accomplished by almost anyone with a limited number of tools and a solid understanding of what steps must be taken.

All this is not what your local contractor would have you believe; obviously, if everyone built his own house there would be no need for carpenters. The truth of the matter is that many people are not confident enough with a hammer and ruler to attempt anything more than hanging a picture. I suspect that this feeling of inadequacy—as a carpenter—comes from lack of familiarity with hand tools and building materials, rather than inability to perform the necessary tasks in any type of building or remodeling project. With this in mind, let's look at how a simple house is constructed.

Because building codes vary from one area to another, it is not possible to give exact dimensional lumber requirements. Dimensional lumber is yard lumber that is nominally 2 or 4 inches thick and 2 or more inches wide. This includes joists, rafters, studs, planks, and small timbers. Building codes are often dictated by the local building department and should be consulted before attempting any remodeling project. Generally speaking, however, the more rural the area, the fewer building codes.

FOUNDATIONS

Every house is built on some type of foundation, usually determined by the local building codes. Foundations can either be a concrete slab, concrete block piers, concrete block walls, reinforced concrete walls, or a combination of these.

Footings act as a base for foundations and transmit the superimposed load to the soil. The type and size of footings should be suitable for the soil condition, and in cold climates the footings should be far enough below ground level to be protected from frost action. Again, local building codes usually establish this depth, which is often 4 feet or more in northern sections of the country.

Footings for piers, posts, or columns should be square and include a pedestal on which the member will rest. A protruding steel pin is ordinarily set in the pedestal to anchor a wood post. Bolts for the bottom plate of steel posts are usually set when the pedestal is poured. At other times, steel posts are set directly on the footing and the concrete is poured around them.

Footings vary in size depending on the allowable soil pressure and the spacing of the piers, posts, or columns. Common sizes are 24 by 24 by 12 inches and 30 by 30 by 24 inches. The pedestal is sometimes poured *after* the footing is poured. The minimum height of the pedestal should be about 3 inches above the finish basement floor and a minimum of 12 inches above finish grade in crawl space areas.

On top of the footings rest either the piers, posts, columns, or walls of either poured concrete or concrete block. Usually, if concrete or block walls are built on top of the footings, 1/2-inch bolts are set into the walls at 8-foot intervals (Fig. 1-1). These bolts are used to anchor the first wooden member of the house—called the sill plate—to the foundation. Anchor bolts are usually embedded 8 inches or more in concrete walls and at least 16 inches in block walls.

The floor framing in a wood-frame house consists specifically of the posts, beams, sill plates, joists, and subfloor (Fig. 1-1). When these are assembled properly on a foundation, they form a level, anchored platform for the rest of the house. The posts and center beams of wood or steel, which support the inside ends of the joists, are sometimes replaced with a wood-frame or masonry wall when the basement area is divided into rooms. Wood-frame houses may also be constructed upon a concrete floor slab or over a crawl space area with floor framing similar to that used for a full basement.

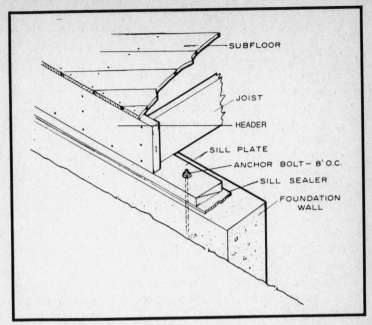

Fig. 1-1. Sill plates are secured to the foundation wall by anchor bolts.

FLOOR FRAMING

On top of the foundation rests a 2-inch (or thicker) sill plate of dimensional lumber. This sill plate is anchored to the top of foundation walls (or piers, columns, etc.) with 1/2-inch bolts set into the foundation. The sill provides support and fastening for the joists and headers. Some houses are constructed without the benefit of an anchored sill plate, although this is not entirely desirable. In such a case, the floor framing should be anchored with metal strapping installed during pouring operations (Fig. 1-2).

Floor joists are selected primarily to meet strength and stiffness requirements. Strength requirements depend upon the loads to be carried. Stiffness requirements place an arbitrary control on the deflection (or bend) of a joist under load. Stiffness also influences the amount of vibration that can be transmitted through joists. Other desirable qualities of floor joists are good nail-holding ability and freedom from warp.

Local building codes usually state the size of dimensional lumber for flooring joists. Wood floor joists are generally of 2 inch (nominal) thickness and of 8, 10, or 12 inch (nominal) depth. The size depends upon the loading, length of span, spacing between joists, and the species and grade of the lumber used.

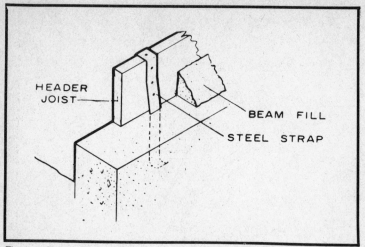

Fig. 1-2. Floor framing can be secured with metal straps.

Span tables for floor joists, which are published by the Federal Housing Administration and local building authorities, can be used as guidelines.

After the sill plates have been anchored to the foundation, the joists are located according to the house design (Fig. 1-3). Sixteen inch center-to-center spacing is most commonly used in wood-frame house construction. Center-to-center (or on-center) is a common building term and is the measurement of spacing between studs, rafters, joists, and the like. Sixteen inches on-center (O.C.) simply means that the distance from the center of one framing member to the center of the next should be 16 inches.

The header joist is fastened to each floor joist with three sixteenpenny nails. In addition, the header joists and stringer joists (Fig. 1-3) are toenailed to the sill with tenpenny nails, also 16 inches on-center. Each floor joist should be toenailed to the sill and center beam with two tenpenny nails; then they are usually nailed to each other (at a center beam) with three or four sixteenpenny nails.

The "in-line" joist system is sometimes used in floor and ceiling framing. This system normally allows the use of one smaller joist size when center supports are present (Fig. 1-4). It makes use of joists of unequal length: Long overhanging joists are cantilevered over the center support; shorter joists are then spliced to the larger ones. Overhang joists are alternated. Depending on the span, species, and joist size, the overhang varies from 1 foot 10 inches to 2 feet 10 inches. Plywood splice plates are used on each side of the joist joints.

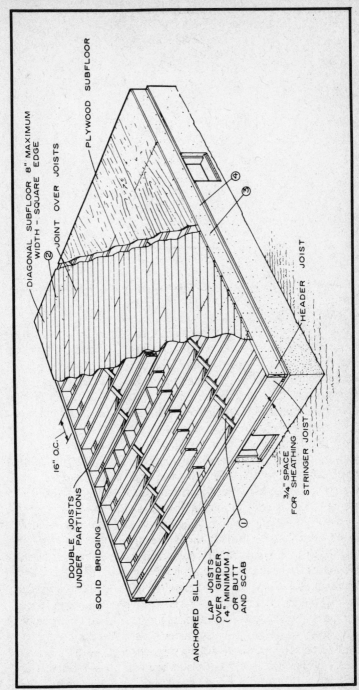

DIAGONAL SUBFLOOR 8" MAXIMUM
WIDTH - SQUARE EDGE

PLYWOOD SUBFLOOR

② JOINT OVER JOISTS

④

③

HEADER JOIST

16" O.C.

DOUBLE JOISTS
UNDER PARTITIONS

SOLID BRIDGING

ANCHORED SILL

LAP JOISTS
OVER GIRDER
(4" MINIMUM)
OR BUTT
AND SCAB

①

3/4" SPACE
FOR SHEATHING

STRINGER JOIST

Fig. 1-3. Conventional platform construction.

13

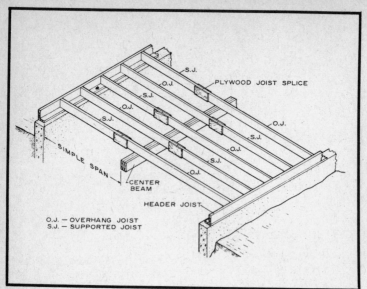

Fig. 1-4. In-line joist system.

SUBFLOORING

Subflooring is used over the floor joists to form a working platform and base for finish flooring (Fig. 1-5). It usually consists of either (1) square-edge or tongue-and-groove boards no wider than 8 inches and not less than 3/4 inch thick or (2) plywood 1/2 to 3/4 inch thick, depending on species, type of finish floor, and spacing of floor joists.

Subflooring boards may be applied either diagonally, which is most common, or at right angles to the floor joists. When subflooring is placed at right angles to the joists, the finish floor should be laid at right angles to the subflooring. Diagonal subflooring permits finish flooring to be laid either parallel or at right angles (most common) to the joists. The subflooring is, of course, nailed to the joists.

Plywood subflooring can be obtained in a number of grades designed to meet a broad range of requirements. All interior grades are available with fully waterproof adhesive identical to those used in exterior plywood. Waterproof grades are useful where a hazard of prolonged moisture exists, such as in underlayments or subfloors adjacent to plumbing fixtures. Under normal conditions, standard sheeting grades are satisfactory for subfloor sheeting.

Plywood suitable for subfloors, such as standard sheeting (Structural I and II, and C-C Exterior grades) has a panel index marking on each sheet (Fig. 1-6). These markings indicate the

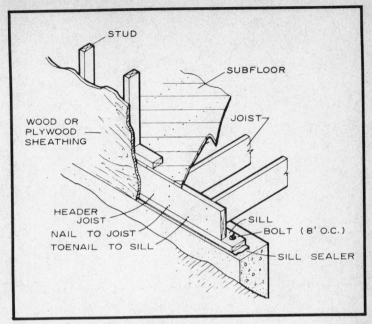

Fig. 1-5. Subfloors are installed onto the floor joists.

allowable spacing for rafters and floor joists when the plywood is used for roof sheathing or subflooring. For example, an index mark of 32/16 indicates that the plywood panel is suitable for a maximum rafter spacing of 32 inches and floor joist spacing of 16 inches. Thus, no problem of strength differences between species is involved because the correct identification is shown on each panel.

Normally, when some type of underlayment is used over the plywood subfloor, the minimum thickness of the subfloor, for

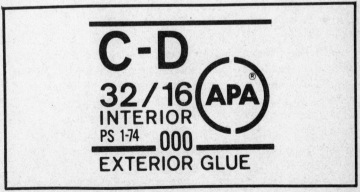

Fig. 1-6. Typical plywood grade marking.

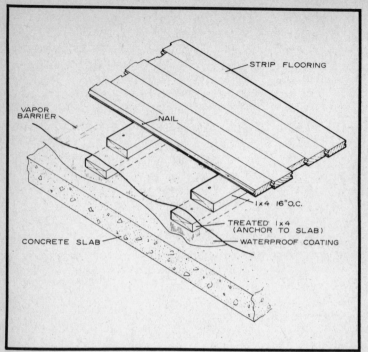

STRIP FLOORING

VAPOR BARRIER

NAIL

1x4 16"O.C.

TREATED 1x4 (ANCHOR TO SLAB)

WATERPROOF COATING

CONCRETE SLAB

Fig. 1-7. Wood "sleepers" fastened to concrete slabs can serve as a base for flooring.

species such as Douglas fir, is 1/2 inch when joists are spaced 16 inches on-center. This thickness of plywood might be used with 24-inch spacing of joists when a 25/32 inch strip finish flooring is installed at right angles to the joists. However, it is important to have a solid and safe platform for workmen during construction of the remainder of the house. For this reason, some builders prefer a slightly thicker plywood subfloor, especially when joist spacing is greater than 16 inches on-center.

Plywood can also serve as combined subfloor and underlayment. The plywood used in this manner must be tongued and grooved or blocked with 2 inch lumber along the unsupported edges.

Plywood should be installed with the grain direction of the outer plies at right angles to the joists and be staggered so that end joints in adjacent panels break over different joists. Plywood should be nailed to the joists with threaded or annular shanked nails. When plywood serves as both subfloor and underlayment, nails should be spaced 6 to 7 inches apart in all directions.

Bridging (Fig. 1-3) is often used when joist length is greater than 8 feet. Sometimes bridging is required by local codes. There are three kinds of bridging: cross, solid, and metal. Cross bridging uses diagonally placed lumber, usually 1 × 4s, crossed to form an X. The tops are nailed, but the bottoms are left loose and nailed only after the flooring is in place and shrinkage is no longer a problem.

Solid bridging uses pieces of dimensional lumber the same width and thickness as joists. Pieces of solid bridging are most commonly staggered to permit end nailing through the joists. One argument against solid bridging is that shrinkage can cause snug-fitting bridges to work loose and thereby lessen their effectiveness.

The third type of bridging involves the use of metal straps nailed on the top of one joist and the bottom of an adjoining joist. Two metal straps are nailed between each joist to form an X similar to the cross bridging with 1 × 4s. Metal bridging is the easier to work with because no cutting is involved; the metal straps come in predetermined lengths. The advantage of bridging with metal straps is that they can be easily tightened after shrinkage takes place in the joists.

The purpose of bridging is to stiffen the joists and minimize any lateral movement. Theoretically this should eliminate any creaking in the finished floor, but there usually is some shrinkage of bridging materials. Nevertheless, bridging is common practice, and you should know what all those Xs are under your floors.

After the subfloor has been fastened down to the joists, it is used as a base or platform for building the rest of the house. Next, the walls are framed, and on top of them rest the ceiling joists, which are also the flooring joists for the rooms above. Then the roof is framed, sheeted, and shingled. Windows, doors, exterior siding are installed next, and then the house is closed in from the weather. Once this takes place, the interior of the house is worked on. Insulation is attached between the studs of the outer walls, interior walls and ceilings are covered with finish material (usually sheetrock), and then the finish flooring is installed.

FINISH FLOORING

Finish flooring is the final covering placed on the floors. There are many choices for finish flooring, including wood, vinyl, asphalt, and ceramic. Cost and installation are usually the factors governing the choice of finish flooring. Table 1-1 can be used as a guide to the differences between types of finish floor coverings. Later chapters cover in depth the various types of finish floor coverings, but I think here might be a good place to briefly describe the different types.

Wood floorings are available in many different varieties in two main categories: hardwood and softwood. Certain hardwoods, be-

Table 1-1. Cost and Characteristics of Common Finish Flooring.

MATERIAL	CHARACTERISTICS	COST PER SQ. FOOT (APPROXIMATE)
Wood strip flooring	Long life	
	Minimum care	
	Moderate resiliency	$0.70 – $1.50
Sheet vinyl	Long life	
	Little care required	
	High resiliency	$0.35 – $4.00
Vinyl tile	Same as sheet vinyl	$0.40 – $4.00
Vinyl-asbestos tile	Same as sheet vinyl	$0.20 – $0.70
Ceramic tile	Very long life	
	No resiliency	
	Little or no care	$0.60 – $2.00

cause of their high resistance to wear, are more often used than others. Two of these are oak and maple.

All wood flooring is finished with a combination of coatings, such as a sealer and varnish, or a liquid plastic. The most common type of liquid plastic is polyurethane; it has either a flat or glossy finish.

Wood flooring may be simply nailed to the subfloor or, when used over a concrete slab, nailed to wood "sleepers" fastened to the slab (Fig. 1-7). In either case, the floor is sanded smooth and finished with stain and sealer.

The most commly used hardwood flooring is oak; it has beauty, warmth, and durability. Maple flooring is produced from the sugar or rock maple. It is smooth, strong, and hard. The grain of maple does not have as much contrast as oak; however, where a smooth polished surface is desired, maple makes a superior floor covering.

Beech, birch, hickory, and several other hardwoods are also sometimes used, but higher costs tend to make these types of hardwood flooring less available. Oak flooring is, generally speaking, more plentiful and therefore in greater use.

Hardwood strip flooring is hollowed or has V-slots cut into its back surface to minimize warping. It is produced in thicknesses of 3/8, 1/2, or 25/32 inch and in widths varying from 1 1/2 to 3 1/4 inches, with the most popular width being 2 1/4 inches. Hardwood strip flooring is tongue and grooved to provide tight-fitting joints.

Hardwood flooring is graded on its appearance according to the number of defects, variations of color, and surface characteristics. Strength and wear are not dependent on grading since all grades are comparable in these respects.

Strip flooring is available prefinished. The finish is applied at the factory, and the floor can be used right after installation. It is available in an imitation peg style, random width, and simulated plank.

Also available is softwood flooring. The softwood most used in this country is southern yellow pine. Douglas fir is next with western hemlock and larch following. Some woods such as redwood, cedar, cypress, and eastern white pine are used in areas where they are common and readily availalbe.

Softwood flooring is available in several sizes and thicknesses; the most common is 25/32 inch thick and 4 1/2 inches wide. The long edges of the flooring are tongue and groove or side matched in order to give tight fitting joints. Similar to hardwood, the underside is hollowed or V grooved to minimize warping.

Hardwood squares 9 × 9 inches or 12 × 12 inches can be purchased to produce a parquet floor. These squares are available in several types of wood such as oak, maple, mahogany, cherry, and teak. They can be 1/2 or 5/16 inch thick.

Thin block flooring is normally produced in prefinished form. The blocks may be nailed to the subfloor or secured with a mastic (a type of waterproof adhesive). These materials, though costing more than strip flooring, require no finishing and are competitive in completed costs.

Sheet vinyl may be produced with a layer of vinyl foam bonded to the backing or between the vinyl finish surface and the backing. The result is a resilient flooring with good walking comfort and an effective sound-absorbant quality (Fig. 1-8).

The vinyl is produced in rolls 8 feet wide or wider and can be installed over most subsurfaces. Though the material has high resistance to grease, stains, and alkali, its surface is easily damaged by abrasion and indentation since it is, generally, a soft product.

Of all the various tiles, vinyl tile is the most costly but also the most wear resistant and the easiest to care for. It is produced in

Fig. 1-8. A sheet vinyl floor.

standard size squares, 9 × 9 inches and 12 × 12 inches, in standard thicknesses of 1/16, 3/32 and 1/8 inch.

Vinyl-asbestos tile consists of blended compositions of asbestos fibers, vinyls, plasticizers, color pigments, and fillers. The most common square sizes are 9 × 9 inches or 12 × 12 inches, with standard thicknesses of 1/16, 3/32, and 1/8 inch. The tile may be obtained in marbleized patterns or textured ones that simulate stone, marble, travertine, and wood.

Vinyl-asbestos tile is semiflexible and requires a rigid subfloor for support. The tile has high resistance to grease, oils, alkaline substances, and some acids. It is quiet underfoot, and many forms can go without waxing for extended periods of time. It can be used almost anywhere and can be obtained with a peel-and-stick backing which makes installation quick and neat.

Nonresilient flooring includes brick pavers, ceramic and clay tile, stone, and terrazzo. These materials are more difficult to install than other flooring materials and usually are the most expensive. However, the long life and durability of nonresilient flooring makes it the choice of people interested in low-maintenance, beautiful floors.

Nonresilient flooring may be installed using a special "thin-set" cement, the traditional 3/4 inch bed of mortar, or with waterproof adhesive. All types of nonresilient flooring require a grout fill between the edges of each tile.

Glazed ceramic tile and terra cotta are relatively nonporous and so resist staining. These glazed tiles are, however, susceptible to scratching and crazing (formation of minute cracks) with age. Ceramic tiles range in size from what is called "mosaic" tile of 3/8 × 3/8 inch to a large 16 × 18 inches.

Mosaic tiles commonly are sold on a backing sheet, making possible the installation of larger areas at one time. Joints between the tiles must, however, be grouted. American Olean, one of the largest tile producers in America, now offers tile sheets that require grouting only between the sheets and not the individual tiles. These new pregrouted sheets greatly simplify and speed up ceramic tile installation.

Unglazed ceramic tile, slate, and flagstone are porous unless treated with a special stain-resistant sealant. Sometimes polyurethane is used.

Clay, or quarry, tile (usually unglazed) is produced from clays and has a strong, long-wearing surface. It is relatively easy to maintain and withstands impact well. Colors are earth tones: reds, buffs, blacks, browns, grays, and gold. A semiglazed type is produced in grays, browns, and greens. Different types of surface patterns and textures are also available. Clay tiles are, generally speaking, the thickest type of tiles, ranging from 1/4 and 1/2 inch up to 1 1/2 inches depending on width and length. They may be square, rectangular, or geometric.

Terrazzo consists of marble chips embedded in portland cement mortar; the surface is ground and polished to a smooth finish. It is very resistant to moisture and therefore relatively easy to maintain.

In the past, most nonresilient flooring was installed in a mortar base, which required more than the average amount of skill. Now, however, modern adhesives have been developed so that almost anyone, with the right approach, can install a tile floor.

Cost of flooring can vary. Your purchase decision should be based on how much you can afford, your ability to work with hand tools and modern flooring materials, and the results you hope to achieve. Later chapters deal, in greater detail, with the finish flooring materials briefly described above. Shop around at local flooring stores for the best buy and ask questions. With the information contained in these pages, you should be able to make a decision about finish flooring that you will be satisfied with.

Chapter 2
Nonceramic Tile Flooring

Nonceramic tile comes in three forms: vinyl, vinyl-asbestos, and asphalt. Of these, vinyl-asbestos is by far the most popular—and the most versatile.

Not too many years ago floor tile was limited to a few rather nondescript colors. Now, however, the range of colors, styles, and patterns can help you create almost any type of atmosphere, from intimate to bold.

BASIC CONSIDERATIONS

Planning is the key to an effective tile floor. Choose colors that you will not tire of easily, colors that harmonize with your furnishings and walls. Remember that neutral or light colors will make your floor appear larger, more open. Cool colors, such as blues and greens, give a room a restful, spacious feeling. The warm colors, reds, browns, beiges, will create a floor that exudes feelings of intimacy and solidity.

The amount of existing natural light should help in choosing the right color for that room. For rooms that receive a lot of natural sunlight, you can use cool greens and blues. Add warmth to rooms with little or no natural lighting by covering the floors with earthy colors, such as brown or the darker greens. Rooms with small windows can be brightened by covering the floors with light-colored tile.

Before you make your final color decision, bear in mind that a complete floor will have more of an impact than a small sample.

Though a tile sample may seem perfect in the store, it could be overpowering when an entire floor is covered. It may be helpful to have the tile salesman lay out several full-sized tiles to give the effect of an installed floor. This will help you visualize the color over a large area. It might also be helpful to bring along samples of your wall and furniture colors to see how the floor tile you have chosen will blend with the rest of the room.

Besides all the colors available, there is also quite a large selection of tile patterns. You may decide on a pattern that looks like weathered wood or one that resembles marble, slate, brick, gravel, travertine, or terrazzo (Fig. 2-1). Some tiles have embossed pat-

Fig. 2-1. Wood-textured vinyl-asbestos floor tile.

terns; others are smooth surfaced, and some have textured surfaces. Whatever your selection, keep in mind how the pattern of tile will coordinate with your existing furnishings.

Another thing to consider when planning a new floor is tile design, or placement. You can create custom floor tile designs straight from the carton and at a very low cost. Floor tile designs should, however, be based on the size and shape of the room. Let simplicity be your guide. You should bear in mind that conservative designs, neutral colors, and even no design pattern at all will permit a greater freedom in decorating the finished room. You should use simple designs in small rooms, but you have more freedom to be bold in larger rooms. Avoid, at all times, a cluttered design, especially in living rooms and bedrooms. Quiet, subtle designs are best for these rooms. But you can add a festive mood to family and game rooms by using more intricate designs. The design will be more effective and attractive if you use your basic tile color over at least 60% of the floor. Also, you should limit your use of color to two or three selections (Fig. 2-2).

After you have resolved what to do with your floor, take some time to ask yourself some important questions about your decorating plans. What kind of traffic flow does the room normally have? Do you want to change this traffic pattern? If so, can the change be made simply by rearranging the existing furnishings? What are the dimensions of the room and what architectural features—windows, built-ins, doors—does it have? What facilities do you have or need for heating, water, air conditioning? How much can you afford to spend on redecorating? The time you spend initially to plan the job thoroughly is a good investment that will save you many headaches when you finally get into the redecorating.

Another point for consideration is the general condition of the existing floor, for this will determine how much surface preparation is necessary. Because all nonceramic flooring conforms to the subfloor on which it is installed, any imperfection or unevenness in the subfloor will be reflected in the finished job. Therefore, a sound, smooth subfloor of concrete or wood is a necessary prerequisite to any floor recovering project.

To determine the number of tiles necessary to cover your floor, you must first measure the room. Measure the length of one wall and multiply this figure by the length of an adjacent wall. The resulting figure is the square footage of the floor space to be covered.

Most nonceramic floor tiles are sold in 12-inch-square pieces, so the number of tiles you will need is the square foot figure. For

Fig. 2-2. Floor tiles don't have to be monochromatic. Two colors are usually better than one.

example, if the dimensions of a room are 12 by 10 feet, the total floor area is 120 square feet. You will need 120 pieces of tile to cover this floor. As insurance, to cover miscuts or other mistakes, you should buy an additional 10% more tiles.

Unless you are installing self-adhesive tile, you will need adhesive for the floor covering job. Most of the major tile manufacturers offer a complete line of adhesives designed for their tile. You should use these recommended adhesives for best results. Basically, there are two types of adhesive for nonceramic tile: hard-set and nonhard-set. The hard-set type dries hard to achieve a bond, while the nonhard-set adhesives set up but never completely harden; they remain flexible and tacky. Specific application and spreading directions are on each adhesive container. These should always be read and followed carefully. You should also buy the proper type of notched trowel for the adhesive you will be applying. This information should be in the directions on the adhesive container.

In addition to tile, adhesive, and trowel, the following tools will also be helpful:

Chalk line

Steel square or *straight edge*—as a guide for cutting

50 foot tape and *6 foot folding rule*—for measuring and laying out

10-inch divider—for scribing irregular shapes

Three-section roller—rent from tile distributor

Hand block plane or *Surform tool*—for leveling high spots on wooden floors

Putty knife—2 or 3 inches wide

Blow torch

Hook knife or *utility knife*—for cutting tile

Steel wool—for cleaning adhesive on face of tile

Awl—for scribing cuts on tile

SURFACE PREPARATION

The purpose of floor surface preparation is to provide a clean, flat, solid surface that will accept the new covering. Good surface preparation is a necessary prerequisite for any floor covering project. The target to aim for when conditioning floors is a flat, level, solid, moisture free, clean area with a relative temperature of no less than 70°F.

Surface preparation is particularly important when installing vinyl tile. Never install vinyl tile on the following types of surfaces:

Single-layer wood subfloors

Particle board

Wood subfloors lying directly on concrete slabs resting on the earth

Wood subfloors that do not have at least 24 inches of ventilation space below

Floors with floor coverings on a wood subfloor (This does not include floors with floor coverings of firmly bonded asphalt tile or vinyl-asbestos tile. But floor coverings of cork, rubber, and linoleum must be removed.)

Wood subfloors with deadening felt or semisaturated felt (Use only thoroughly saturated asphalt felt.)

Unprimed new wood subfloors (Shellac or other wood sealers lessen the tendency of boards to cup.)

Because all vinyl tile conforms to the subfloor on which it is laid, any imperfections or unevenness in the subfloor will be reflected in the finished job. Therefore, it is important to begin the installation with a carefully and properly prepared subfloor. In most cases vinyl tile can be installed on either concrete or wooden subfloors.

Preparing Concrete Subfloors

All concrete subfloors, above or below grade, must be cleaned of all foreign matter such as wax, paint, grease, or oil. New concrete must be properly cured, preferably by covering with polyethylene film. Under ideal conditions a drying time of at least 8 weeks is generally required after the slab has been poured and protected from the weather. Lightweight aggregate concrete floors and floors with steel or plastic pan construction usually require an extended drying time. If lightweight aggregate concrete weighs less than 90 pounds per cubic foot, a topping of regular concrete at least 1 inch thick is required.

Before installing a new nonceramic tile floor on a concrete slab, any alkali remaining in the concrete must be neutralized. This can be accomplished by thoroughly rinsing the floor with clear water several times to remove all traces of alkali. If there is a drain in the floor, it is advisable to rinse the floor with a hose. Considerable rinsing is required to remove all alkali.

After the floor is rinsed, it must be washed with a 10% solution of muriatic acid and clear water (nine parts water to one part muriatic acid). The rinse the floor again and allow to dry for several days.

Caution: Wear goggles, rubber shoes, and rubber gloves when working with muriatic acid. If contact with skin, wash thoroughly with water immediately.

After the floor has been thoroughly rinsed and dried, you can perform a simple test to make sure that all the alkali has been removed from the cement. Make a 2% solution of phenolphthalein dissolved in alcohol; a 1-ounce bottle is sufficient and can be purchased at any drug store. Put about one teaspoonful of water on different areas of the floor around the room; then place a few drops of the phenolphthalein solution on the wet spots, using an eye dropper. If these spots turn pink, red, or purple, the alkali has not been neutralized, which will necessitate repeating the above treatment with muriatic acid solution.

Old concrete subfloors must be cleaned of all paint, varnish, grease, or wax, and all uneven places must be leveled by chipping or filling. All expansion joints, grooves, cracks, potholes, etc. must be filled, and the subfloor must be uniformly smooth, level, and solid before installing tile.

In some instances, paint may be removed with a sanding machine using an open-coat sandpaper. This method is not too effective on or below grade because paint may remain in the pores of the concrete and upon exposure may react on the cement causing it to bleed at the tile joints.

The cheapest and most effective method for removing paint, varnish, wax, or grease is with an application of a strong solution of industrial lye or caustic soda. When the solution is spread over the surface with a brush or broom, agitate it every few minutes with a brush or broom until the paint or other coating has been dissolved. Spread sawdust or dry sand over the area to absorb as much of the solution as possible, then shovel it out. Rinse the floor thoroughly and neutralize the alkaline surface with an acid solution as outlined above.

Never use compounds or solutions containing solvents to remove oil, grease, paint, etc. from concrete subfloors, the solvent may be absorbed by the concrete and after installation return to the surface to soften tile and adhesive.

Preparing Wood Subfloors

A wood subfloor must be at least 18 inches above ground level and be well ventilated before you can expect a problemless floor. Wood subfloors must be of double construction—that is, a layer of rough wood flooring covered by a top layer of strip wood flooring. If your floor is of single wood construction, or it is rough and worn double wood, it can be made suitable for the installation of tile with an underlayment of plywood. Paint, oil, varnish, and wax must be removed from old wood floors before installing tile. Wood subfloors should be sanded or scraped to a uniform smooth surface. If boards are over 2 inches wide, prime with a light coat of shellac or other wood sealer to lessen the tendency of cupping due to absorption of moisture. Wood subfloors should not contain any cupped, springy, loose, or rotten boards. Replace or nail down where necessary.

There are two possible solutions for problem wood floors: cover with fully saturated asphalt felt, or cover with plywood underlayment. In cases where the floor is sound, except for small spaces between the flooring boards, asphalt felt can be used to provide a flat surface for the tile. But where the subfloor is uneven, rough, worn, or with boards less than 4 inches wide, it must be covered with 1/4-inch plywood or masonite underlayment board. In either case, make sure that all wax, grease, dirt, and dust are off the floor. Be sure the wood floor is solid, well nailed at joists, and free from spring. Smooth over any unevenness with a sanding machine. Small high spots on wooden floors can often be leveled with a small block plane (Fig. 2-3).

If, after you have made the floor as uniform as possible, you decide to cover it with asphalt felt, begin as follows. Lay 15-pound

Fig. 2-3. The appearance of any finish flooring will depend a great deal on the condition of the subfloor.

Fig. 2-4. Butt underlayment sheets together.

thoroughly saturated asphalt felt at right angles to the floor boards. Fit the asphalt felt to the entire floor area, closely butting, but not overlapping, the edges of the paper. Then roll all sheets half way back, leaving half the floor area open for application of linoleum paste.

Spread linoleum paste with a properly notched trowel to cement the felt to the wood subfloor. Carefully replace the felt into its original position. Then roll back the other half of the sheets, apply paste, and replace into original position, using care to see that sheets are properly butted but not overlapped. Next roll the felt with a three-section roller in several directions to assure complete adhesion and removal of air pockets.

If you decide that you must cover your floor with plywood or Masonite boards, proceed as follows (after you have made the necessary repairs and sanded or fastened down any rambunctious boards). Plywood (underlayment grade APA) is recommended by the American Plywood Association as the most suitable plywood base for resilient flooring. On boards 4 inches or wider, use 3/8- or 1/2-inch plywood. Use waterproof plywood wherever there is any danger of moisture—under refrigerators, vegetable counters, sinks, or bathroom fixtures. Also use waterproof plywood if the wood subfloor is over a damp area, such as the first floor with no provision for heat in the basement underneath.

Next, lay the underlayment sections snugly (whether plywood or Masonite) (Fig. 2-4). Leave a space, about the thickness of a paper matchbook cover, to allow for possible expansion between the sheets of underlayment (Fig. 2-5). The joints between the boards should be broken at the midpoint of the adjoining board.

Nail the plywood or Masonite underlayment with coated or ring-shanked nails every 4 inches over the entire face of the panels and every 2 inches at the edges. When nailing underlayment board, start at the center and work toward the edges so that no wrinkling or buckling will occur.

The use of particle board, chipboard, flakeboard, etc. is not approved as a suitable underlayment for the installation of most manufacturers' tile. There are many brands of such materials offered as underlayment for resilient tile flooring; however, since these vary widely in their performance, most manufacturers will not assume responsibility for flooring failures where such underlayment materials have been used.

LAYING THE TILE

Tile must be laid from the center of the room outward; you should never start along a wall. And finding dead center can't be left to guesswork. Your measurements must be exact, on the money. So start by measuring the length of a principal wall, disregarding wall offsets and alcoves. Divide the measurement by two to find the center point; drive a nail at this mark. Repeat this whole process for the opposite wall. Snap a chalk line between the two nails and measure along the line to find the middle of the room (Fig. 2-6).

Once you've pinpointed the room's center, you've got to draw another guideline through it so the tile can be laid squarely. To no

Fig. 2-5. Allow a little less than 1/32 inch (the thickness of a paper matchbook) between each panel.

one's surprise, this job is sometimes referred to as squaring the floor area. At the room's center point, draw a line perpendicular to the first; extend it from wall to wall. You can use a carpenter's square to make sure that the second line is at right angles to the first (Fig. 2-7).

Another way to establish a line that is exactly at right angles to the first chalk line is to use a 3-4-5 triangle. Along the first line, measure 4 feet toward each side wall from the center point (Fig. 2-8). Mark these points. Then measure 3 feet from the center point along the first line. Mark this point. Measure exactly 5 feet from the 3-foot point on the first line to the 4-foot marks. Mark the spots where the 5-foot lines intersect the 4-foot points. A line through these two spots will be at right angles to the first guideline. Now snap your chalk line across the two points and the middle point. For larger rooms, multiples of the 3-4-5 triangle may be used to obtain greater accuracy (6-8-10, 9-12-15, etc.).

Now that the floor has been perfectly squared (and the room has been divided into four parts) you can begin laying one test row of uncemented tile from the center point to one side wall and to one end wall. These two rows of tile are laid along the chalk lines, as in Fig.

Fig. 2-6. Connect the two nails with a chalk line.

Fig. 2-7. Use a carpenter's square to draw a second line perpendicular to the first.

2-9, and will indicate how the last tile, the one next to the wall, will fit. If the resulting border is too small, less than one half tile, move the starting point over one-half tile width so that it straddles the centerline. Repeat the same procedure lengthwise in the room.

After the proper border widths have been determined and the guidelines are moved, if necessary, spread the recommended adhesive over one of the four parts of the room. Spread the adhesive just past the guidelines; the guidelines can be resnapped later (Fig. 2-10). Allow the adhesive to dry hard enough so it will not absorb chalk when the new line is snapped. It should take about 15 minutes for the adhesive to dry. Test the cement for proper tackiness by touching with the thumb. It should feel tacky but should not stick to the thumb. If it sticks to the thumb, allow more drying time. When the adhesive is just right, resnap the guidelines using the original, uncovered lines as a guide.

Next, start laying the tile from the centerpoint outward (Fig. 2-11). Always refer to your guidelines as you progress so that any mistake can be corrected before it gets out of hand. Make sure each tile is butted against adjoining tiles, but do not *slide* tiles into place. It may be necessary, at times, to compromise on the tightness of joints between the tile because of unevenness or waves in the subfloor. When laying simulated-marble tile, the direction of tile marbling should be reversed in adjoining tile. Generally speaking, it is never necessary to heat any field (nonborder) tile. Always work ahead of yourself from the finished floor, using care to prevent skidding of the tile on which you are kneeling. Border tiles should be installed only after the field tiles have been completely laid.

To accurately mark border tiles, place a loose tile (Fig. 2-12A) squarely on top of the last full tile closest to the wall. On top of this, place another tile (B) and slide it until it butts against the wall. Using the edge of the top tile as a guide, mark the tile under it (A) with a

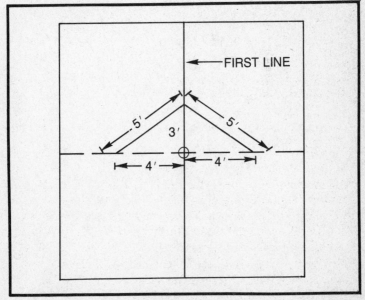

Fig. 2-8. You can use a 3-4-5 triangle to draw a line perpendicular to another.

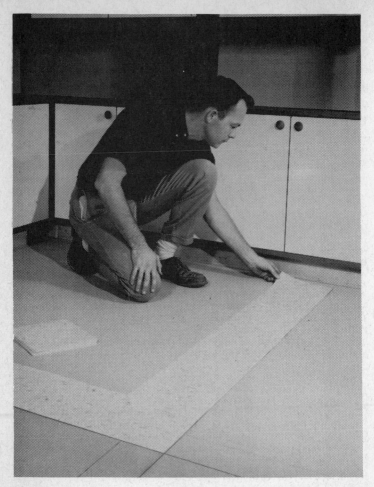

Fig. 2-9. Lay one test row of uncemented tile along the chalk lines.

pencil. Next, with a pair of household shears, cut the marked tile (A) along the pencil line (Fig. 2-13). After the tile has been cut, place it into the adhesive along the wall.

To fit tiles around doorways, pipes, heaters, and other irregular shapes, make a paper pattern to fit the space exactly. Then trace the outline of the paper onto the tile and cut with a pair of household shears or utility knife. After cutting, sand off rough edges with sandpaper or suitable file. Press the tile into place (Fig. 2-14).

After the first quarter of the floor has been completely covered with tile, repeat the same procedure for the next three. When the entire floor has been covered with tile, roll the floor with a 150-pound roller to assure a tight bond. The dealer who sells you the tile should be able to loan or rent you a roller. If you can't borrow or rent a 150-pound roller, you can use an ordinary household rolling pin. This rolling step is optional with 1/16-inch gauge tile but recommended with 1/8-inch gauge tile.

After you have finished the job of laying the tile, look over the work and check for spots of adhesive that may have oozed out from under the tile. If you find any, and it is still wet, it can be removed with a damp cloth. If dry, it can be removed with fine steel wool. Never use solvents.

Do not wash or wax the new floor for 7 days. This period will give the tiles sufficient time to become thoroughly bonded to the

Fig. 2-10. Spread the adhesive just past the guidelines. Use your thumb to test for proper tackiness.

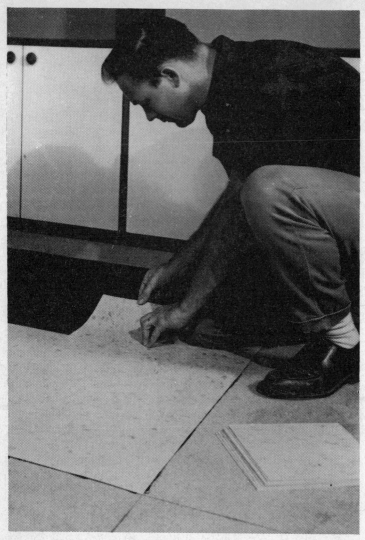

Fig. 2-11. Start from the center of the room and press the tiles into the cement.

subfloor. Sweeping with a soft broom or cleaning with a damp cloth or mop is the only maintenance necessary during this period. After the 7-day setting up period, you may wash and wax the new floor.

MAINTAINING THE NONCERAMIC TILE FLOOR

Wax only a clean, dry tile floor. Do not use paste wax or waxes containing petroleum solvents; such waxes are harmful to asphalt tile floors and do not perform satisfactorily on vinyl floors. To prevent wax buildup, put the wax in a shallow container, dip wax applicator in wax, press out, and apply wax from a damp, not wet, applicator. Spread the wax thinly and evenly, making long straight strokes in one direction only. Wait 30 minutes for the wax to dry before walking on the floor and 2 hours before applying a second coat. Remember that two light coats of wax are better than one heavy coat. Buff the floor for a higher gloss, when the wax has dried. To buff, use a clean weighted cloth or polishing machine. Use a soft Tampico fiber brush on the machine, not steel wool pads. Frequent buffing rather than frequent waxing gives luster to your floor and prevents wax buildup.

Protect your floors from marks and dents with proper furniture rests. Furniture legs of small diameter concentrate too much weight on one spot. Furniture rests with broad bases spread the weight over a larger area and prevent mars and dents. The rests you choose should be flat and smooth, with round edges to prevent cutting. For side chairs, small cabinets, and frequently moved small pieces of furniture, use glides or rollers with smooth, flat-base rounded edges and flexible pins to maintain flat contact with the floor. Size will

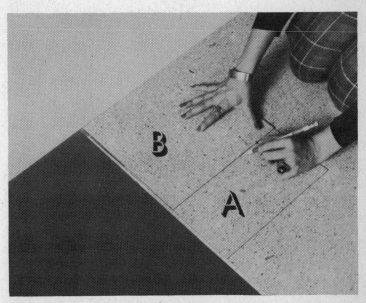

Fig. 2-12. Place a loose tile (A) squarely on top of the full tile closest the wall. On top of this, place a third tile (B), butting it firmly against the wall. Use B as a straightedge to draw a line across A with a pencil.

Fig. 2-13. Tiles can be cut with household shears.

depend on the weight of the piece of furniture. Remove small metal domes from bottoms of furniture legs and replace with flat guides.

For large, heavy pieces of furniture, such as couches and china cabinets, which are almost never moved, use composition furniture cups to prevent legs from cutting the floor. Remove metal cones and replace with wide-bearing furniture cups. If the piece of furniture has a large base, which distributes the weight of the piece over a large area, no protection is needed.

For chairs and movable furniture the best protection is easy-swiveling, ball bearing, rubber tread casters or flat guides. Casters should have large diameter wheels (about 2 inches) with soft rubber treads. Hard wheel casters with small diameter and crowned tread will mark resilient floors and should therefore be replaced.

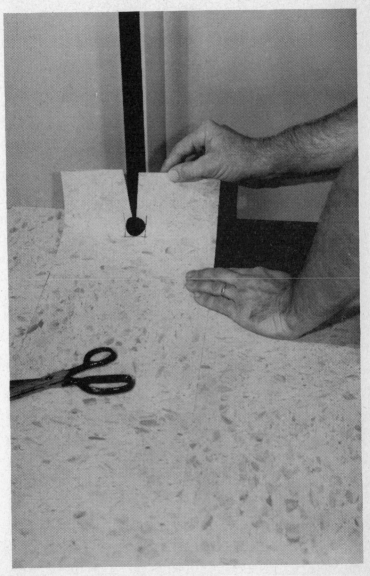

Fig. 2-14. Cut the tile with shears, then press it around the obstruction.

Taking care of vinyl-asbestos tile floors is easy. If you spill something, wipe it up right away before it gets sticky or hard. Taking a few seconds at the time will save you minutes later when the spill has dried and is harder to remove. It makes good sense to sweep your floor daily to remove loose dirt and grit before it has a chance to become ground in. All that is necessary is to go over the floor with a soft broom or dust mop. If accumulated dirt is not removed by sweeping, mop the floor with clear water. But use water sparingly—never flood your floor. Part of the beauty of a vinyl-asbestos floor is that it makes housework easier. Normal daily care and a thorough washing several times a year are all that are necessary to keep your floors bright and shining.

Avoid harmful cleaners. Cleaners containing caustics, harsh soaps, powders, gasoline, kerosene, naphtha, turpentine, and benzene are harmful to resilient floors and should not be used. Oil-base cleaners can damage asphalt floor tile.

Light scratches can be removed by scrubbing with a lukewarm solution of special vinyl cleaner. Most tile companies have a line of cleaners and waxes made specially for their product. Heavier scratches or cigarette burns are removed by rubbing with No. 00 steel wool dipped in vinyl cleaners. In all cases, rinse, dry, and polish. To repair deep cuts and gouges, it is usually necessary to replace the tile. This is a good reason to save any leftover tile.

To remove a damaged tile it is usually best to work with a putty knife from the center of the damaged tile towards the edges. Work carefully when removing the tile so as not to damage surrounding tiles. After the broken tile has been removed, scrape off as much of the old adhesive as possible, sand flat the area, then apply a light coat of new adhesive. Next you must fit the new tile into the space as carefully as possible. There may be a slight color difference, but in time this will disappear.

Plan your floor remodeling project carefully, work conscientiously, and you should have an attractive floor that will shine for years.

Chapter 3
Sheet Vinyl Floors

When most people think of a sheet vinyl floor, the first thing that comes to mind is linoleum. While some linoleum can still be found in dealers' showrooms, eventually none will be left because linoleum isn't being made anymore. After 114 years of production by various manufacturers, linoleum has finally been put out to pasture to make room for newer and better sheet floor coverings.

LINOLEUM AND SHEET VINYL

The name *linoleum* actually refers to one particular type of floor covering invented in 1863 by an Englishman, Frederick Walton. Linoleum flooring is a mixture of oxidized linseed oil, a resin flux, and filler (either ground cork or wood flour) pressed into sheets over burlap or canvas backing and cured for about a week in an oven.

Linoleum enjoyed widespread popularity until after World War II when flooring manufacturers began producing vinyl floor coverings. Since World War II vinyl floors have dominated the market, and the demand for old-fashioned linoleum has been declining. And for good reason; vinyls are more attractive and easier to maintain than linoleum and are just as durable (Fig. 3-1). The final curtain fell on linoleum with the advent of no-wax floors with a glossy wear surface.

The last American linoleum manufacturer, Armstrong, recently stopped making linoleum after continuous production since 1909. In 65 years, Armstrong turned out almost a billion square yards of linoleum—enough to pave a 6-foot wide path from here to the moon and complete four lunar orbits.

Fig. 3-1. A linoleum floor (left); a sheet vinyl floor (right).

Modern vinyl floors are far superior to linoleum floors for several reasons. Vinyl floors are produced in a myriad of designs with bright and sophisticated styles that cannot be matched by linoleum. Cushioned vinyl floors offer quiet, warmth, and comfort underfoot, something that linoleum can never do. Linoleum is restricted in where it can be used. It can't be installed in the basement, for example, a popular recreation area that's perfect for most vinyl floors. Most important, linoleum requires relatively frequent cleaning and waxing to keep it shining. Vinyl floors need less upkeep; they stay sparkling clean with a minimum of mopping and only occasional waxing (Fig. 3-2).

So there you have it—linoleum is no longer being made in America. It has been replaced by modern vinyl flooring, and the change is for the best. Do-it-yourself floors abound in variety, including 9- and 12-foot-wide sheets. Any reasonably handy person can install sheet vinyl flooring and save significantly on costs.

Among the vinyl floor coverings, there are the modern "inlaid" products whose patterns extend from the surface all the way through to the backing for long wearing beauty. There are cushioned vinyls with a feel that might be compared to carpet. Another popular category is the rotovinyls, so termed because they are made by a rotogravure printing process. Because this process involves reproducing a photographed image, a wide variety of patterns can be duplicated with a high degree of realism.

All of these vinyl floors give good service, are styled for today's decorating tastes, and represent major steps forward in the evolution of resilient floors. But most of them lack the high luster that wax imparts. Actually, wax serves two important functions. First, wax puts a shine on the floor. And second, wax helps maintain the shine on shiny-finish vinyls.

Everyone knows that wax makes floor surfaces glisten and gleam. But few people understand the protective power of wax.

Fig. 3-2. Vinyl floors are almost maintenance free.

Fig. 3-3. Sheet vinyl can simulate natural floor coverings.

Without a wax coating, the surface of most vinyl floors can be easily scuffed and scratched. Scratches trap dirt, making cleaning difficult. The shine starts to fade, and permanent damage to the floor can result.

However, Armstrong's Solarian type of floor keeps its shine far longer than most vinyl floors. The glossy Mirabond finish is easy to clean. Sweeping or vacuuming, sponge mopping with warm water, and an occasional detergent washing will keep the floor bright and shiny for quite a while. Eventually, however, even a Solarian floor may require touching up in areas where heavy foot traffic has gradually reduced the gloss.

Vinyl floors can go anywhere; you are not limited (as with the old linoleum floors) by where in the home you can install a new floor. These days virtually every resilient floor material can be installed from attic to basement. The exceptions are the very low-priced vinyl floor coverings and carpeting or rugs that don't have moisture-resistant backings.

There are hundreds of vinyl flooring designs. Perhaps the most popular are those that capture the look of natural materials, such as wood, stone, brick, glazed ceramic tile, and even hand-tooled leather (Fig. 3-3). Other designs have low key patterns, serving more as background for other furnishings. Additionally, almost every color combination that you can imagine can be found at your local floor covering dealer.

TOOLS AND MATERIALS

Estimating the required size of vinyl sheet flooring is quite simple. Sheets are available in 6-, 9-, and 12-foot-wide pieces in almost any length you will need. In most rooms a 12-foot-wide sheet will cover the floor entirely and therefore eliminate the need for seams. Before you pay a visit to the flooring dealer, measure the size of the room you are planning to cover. Remember that the basic idea is to try to cover a floor area with one piece of vinyl. For example, your kitchen's basic dimensions may be 10 by 12 feet. But let's say that because of the cabinets the floor is only 8 feet wide in one area. To have a floor with no seams you must purchase the sheet vinyl for the largest dimensions of the room. Therefore, in this case, you would need one sheet of vinyl, 10 by 12 feet.

In addition to the vinyl, you will also need adhesive or a staple gun with enough staples to fasten down the vinyl. In most cases, sheet vinyl is attached only around the perimeter; therefore, you will not require very much adhesive. Speak to the flooring dealer and he will explain just how much adhesive you will need to install a new sheet vinyl flooring.

A few simple tools are necessary for the installation of sheet vinyl floors:

Chalk line
Utility knife or *strong shears*
Extension ruler or *tape*
Straightedge or *carpenter's square*
Putty knife or *trowel*
Pry bar
Screwdriver
Hammer

SURFACE PREPARATION

Modern sheet vinyl flooring can be installed over existing floor coverings, providing the old covering is flat, clean, and free of holes larger than the diameter of a dime. Sheet vinyl can be installed over almost any kind of surface: particle board, plywood, concrete, terrazzo, marble, ceramic tile, and any resilient floor except another cushioned vinyl. Because it is in sheet form, vinyl flooring has the ability to bridge minor surface irregularities and thereby eliminate most subfloor surface preparation.

Begin surface preparation by removing everything that is movable from the room. Chairs, tables, area rugs, standing lamps, etc. Then remove the baseboard molding around the entire room. This can be done quickly with a pry bar, screwdriver, or putty knife. Work carefully so you don't damage fragile quarter-round or toe molding; such molding must be replaced after the new flooring has been installed. As you pry each piece of molding loose, remove any nails that are still in the piece. This will make the re-installation of the moldings go quicker. Store the nail-free moldings in another room where they will be out of your way while you work on the floor.

After the moldings have been removed and stored elsewhere, you should check the wall area where the moldings were to see if any nails remain. If you find any, remove them. Next check the existing floor surface. Look for nailheads that may have worked up. All nailheads must be flush with the floor surface.

Now check for holes, gouges, or missing sections in the old flooring. These areas must be patched with an appropriate filler. Generally, the best way to fill recesses in the old flooring is to cut out a square of flooring from around the recess and patch in a new square made from the old flooring. If the recess is small enough, it can usually be filled with plastic wood, wood putty, or other suitable filler. You can make your own filler for small holes by mixing equal amounts of white household glue and sawdust. Mix thoroughly, then press into the hole to be filled. After the patched area has dried, it should be sanded flat so it is flush with the rest of the subfloor or existing flooring.

High spots, other than nailheads, should be sanded flat. This can be accomplished with an electric sander (belt or rotary) which can be rented from the flooring dealer. The perimeter of old resilient flooring should be sanded lightly to provide a good base for the adhesive which will be used to attach the new flooring.

After all the necessary surface preparation has been completed and the floor is reasonably flat, you should clean the floor with soap and water. This will remove any dirt or built-up grime that could prevent the adhesive from doing its job. After the floor has been cleaned, it should be vacuumed to pick up anything that might damage the new flooring.

LAYING VINYL FLOORING

The next step is to draw an accurate sketch of the floor which will be receiving the new floor covering. This sketch should include the dimensions of the floor; it will be your guide to cutting the new floor from the solid vinyl sheet (Fig. 3-4). The sketch should include counters, bays, alcoves, appliances, and any other features which will affect the shape and size of the new floor covering.

Fig. 3-4. Measure the floor to be covered, then transfer these dimensions to your sketch.

Fig. 3-5. The flooring can be cut with a utility knife.

Before installation, for a period of at least 24 hours, the new sheet vinyl flooring should lie flat in another room in the house. This will give the new vinyl flooring a chance to acclimate itself to the temperature of the house. The ideal temperature for laying sheet vinyl is between 65° and 75°F. Under no circumstances should you attempt to install sheet vinyl on a floor with a temperature less than 55°.

Transfer the dimensions to the face of the new vinyl flooring, adding 3 inches to all measurements. The extra inches will allow for mistakes in measuring or irregularities of the existing floor. The excess vinyl is trimmed off just before fastening the new flooring.

The initial rough cutting of the new flooring can be easily accomplished with a pair of heavy-duty household shears or a sharp utility (razor) knife (Fig. 3-5). Be sure that the cutting area is free of dirt and grit. Work slowly and carefully to avoid miscuts. It is impossible to put sheet vinyl back together once it has been cut, so bear this in mind.

After the new vinyl has been cut to size (plus 3 inches all around), roll it up and carry it into the room where it will be laid.

Position the new flooring in the room. Fit the excess material into the room corners and make upward cuts at the corners with a utility knife. This will allow the new flooring to flash neatly up the walls and make the job of trimming easier.

Start fitting along the walls first. Use a metal straightedge to press the new flooring into the joint where the wall meets the floor (Fig. 3-6). Use the straightedge as a guide for trimming off the excess flooring. In trimming, a minimum clearance of 1/8 inch must be allowed between the edge of the material and each wall; this clearance allows for expansion and contraction of the new flooring. Most modern sheet vinyl flooring actually moves with the subfloor. The reason that a subfloor expands and contracts is the changes in humidity that are present in every home. The maximum gap allowable is slightly less than the thickness of the baseboard which will be used to cover the edges of the flooring.

If the wall/floor joint is not straight, it may be necessary to curve the flooring material up and trim accordingly. This is where the excess flooring comes in handy. It is important to keep in mind that you must adjust the entire sheet of flooring so the lines or patterns (if any) will run parallel to adjoining walls.

Continue fitting and cutting the new flooring around the entire room until it has been completely cut to size. Once you are satisfied with the fit, you can staple the edges of the new flooring with a heavy-duty staple gun loaded with 3/8- to 9/16-inch staples. Space the staples approximately 3 inches apart (Fig. 3-7).

There will probably be some areas where it will not be possible to staple the new flooring, under counters and cabinets for example. Or possibly you are not planning to install molding to cover the staple heads. One other case in which staples cannot be used is when the subfloor is concrete. In any event, where staples cannot be used, the

Fig. 3-6. Trim the excess flooring off with a straightedge and utility knife.

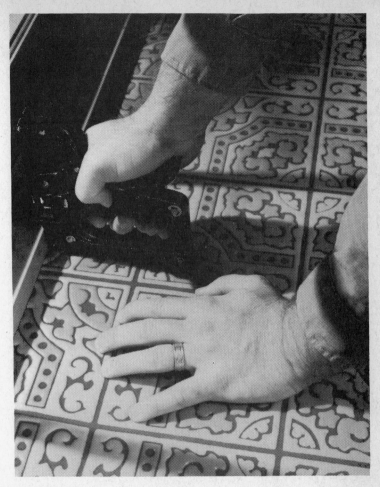

Fig. 3-7. Staple the flooring down with a heavy-duty staple gun.

new flooring can be fastened to the subfloor with adhesive. Simply fold back the new trimmed flooring and apply a few beads of adhesive to the edges of the subfloor (Fig. 3-8). After the adhesive has been applied, fold the flooring back into place and press the area to insure a solid bond.

Adhesive is not applied to areas other than the edges of the subfloor. As I mentioned, sheet vinyl expands and contracts according to the humidity changes in the house. By fastening only the edges of the vinyl, you are insuring that the subfloor is free to move according to humidity changes while the finish floor remains fairly stable. Also, by applying adhesive (or staples) only on the edges of the new flooring, you are cutting investment in both time and materials. One other advantage of attaching only the edges of sheet vinyl is for people who live in apartments or rented houses where permanent changes or improvements are frowned upon. If need be, sheet vinyl that has only been attached around the edges can be removed if you should decide to move or remodel in the future.

After the new flooring has been fastened to the subfloor, you can finish the job by reinstalling the moldings around the entire room. Clearance must be allowed between the sheet vinyl and wooden moldings to allow the walls and subfloor to expand without affecting the vinyl flooring. Wooden moldings should be renailed to the wall (not the floor) after inserting a scrap of flooring between the molding and the floor. Removing the scrap will allow proper clearance. Rubber or vinyl covebase can be cemented back to the wall without clearance (Fig. 3-9). Install a metal threshold molding at doorways, fastening it to the subfloor but not through the new sheet vinyl.

Slack or wrinkles in the flooring caused by slightly inaccurate cutting should disappear after a few hours. After installation, the floor, because of its elasticity, gently contracts, returning to its original dimensions before it was rolled. The sheet vinyl will actually, in a few hours, conform to the contours of the subfloor. This action assures a tight, smooth fit.

CARING FOR VINYL FLOORS

Your new vinyl floor will look better and last longer if it is maintained according to the directions offered by the manufacturer. The Armstrong Cork Company has some timely advice on floor care in their brochure, "How To Keep Your Armstrong Floor Looking Its Best." This publication can be obtained by writing to Armstrong Cork Company, Consumer Services Section, Lancaster, Pennsylvania, 17604.

What follows are some tips on proper care of your sheet vinyl floor.

If the floor is near an outside door, place a mat or throw rug at the entrance to keep soil from being tracked in. The mat or rug should not have synthetic foam backing which might cause the floor to become discolored.

Floor protectors should be used on the legs of furniture to minimize scratches and indentations.

Preventive maintenance requires regular sweeping or vacuuming, sponge mopping with warm water, occasional washing, waxing, and polishing (except in the case of no-wax floors).

Fig. 3-8. Secure the edges of the flooring with adhesive.

To wash vinyl floors, first prepare a cleaning solution with warm water and a general-purpose liquid detergent. Do not use soap-based products which can leave a dulling film on the floor. Use one sponge mop and bucket to wash the floor and another mop and bucket for rinsing. Floors should always be rinsed thoroughly because any detergent left after washing will attract and hold dirt. Dip the sponge mop into the cleaning solution, and without wringing it out, spread it on a small area of the floor—about 3 by 3 feet. Give the detergent a minute or so to attack the dirt, then go over the area with the saturated mop, scrubbing hard enough to clean the floor thoroughly. Stubborn marks can be removed with a nylon scrub pad. Wring out the mop; soak up as much of the cleaning solution as possible.

Next, take your rinse mop, dip it into clear warm water, wring it out, and remove the cleaning solution from the floor. Repeat this procedure, of washing and rinsing an area at a time, over the entire floor. Be sure to change your rinse water often to avoid redepositing any dirt or detergent.

With the exception of no-wax floors, all floors should receive regular applications of a protective floor wax to prevent scratching and to provide a bright shine. Always apply the wax to a clean surface. Follow the steps outlined above for washing, then allow the floor to dry. Apply the wax in a thin, uniform coat. Move the applicator in all directions to assure an even distribution. Remember that two light coats of wax are much better than one heavy coat. Allow sufficient drying time between coats. Let the wax completely dry before using the room, usually about 1/2 hour will be sufficient.

After six or seven waxings it may be necessary to strip the floor of the accumulated layers of wax. This should be done to all vinyl floors, except no-wax type, at least once a year. Several companies make floor wax strippers. Follow the directions on the container, then rinse the floor with clear water. After stripping, the floor is waxed in the usual manner.

No-wax floors should have a bright, shiny appearance to begin with and should keep that shine without waxing far longer than ordinary vinyl floors. To keep that shiny new look, no-wax floors must be swept, sponge-mopped and washed, but not waxed.

Eventually, normal foot traffic may begin to reduce the gloss of a no-wax surface. A special finish available from flooring dealers can be used from time to time to touch up areas that have lost some of their shine—doorways, for example.

Besides periodic maintenance, you should keep after your floor constantly by wiping up spills when they happen. Remember that no

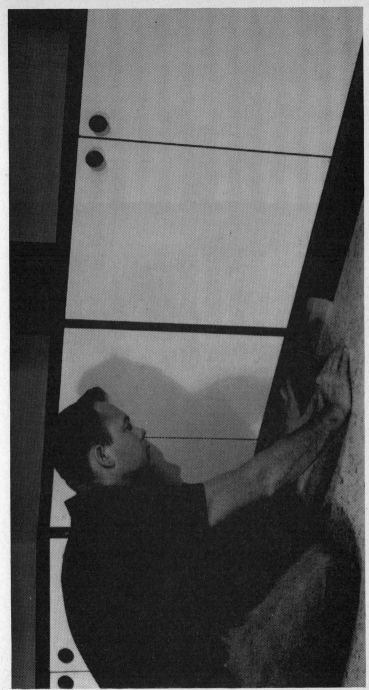

Fig. 3-9. Cement the covebase to the wall.

sheet vinyl floor is completely stainproof. Wipe up the following materials as soon as possible: solvent type shoe polishes, hair waving and dyeing solutions, lipstick and wax crayon marks, furniture oils and polishes, and animal excretions. Pick up burning cigarettes promptly; no vinyl floor can withstand the 1200° temperature of a cigar or cigarette.

There is corollary to all these maintenance considerations. Buy from a reputable dealer and be sure to ask for full maintanence instructions as well as a printed copy of the manufacturer's warranty. Federal law now requires a manufacturer to specify whether his flooring comes with full or limited warranty. Insist on a brand with a full one-year warranty.

Chapter 4
Ceramic Tile Floors

Ceramic tile floors are on the move. Traditionally limited to the bathroom, now ceramic tile floors are common in kitchens, hallways, foyers, and even living rooms (Fig. 4-1). It's not surprising. The almost maintenance-free durability of ceramic tile makes it a good choice for high-traffic areas. And with the wide choice of colors, patterns, and styles, you can create a tile floor that is unique and tough as stone.

THE FACTS ABOUT CERAMIC TILE

Obviously, ceramic tile floors cost more than sheet vinyl or vinyl-asbestos tile, but the extra investment will pay off in the long run. For example, if you should have to sell your home, ceramic tile can increase your property value. Then there is the matter of aesthetics. Just about every other type of floor covering is an imitation of real ceramic tile. But the truth is that ceramic tile will last ten times longer than any vinyl and still look beautiful.

With ceramic tile you don't have to worry about surfaces that fade, warp, scorch, cut, stain, or burn. It's not indestructible, but ceramic tile does stand up to traffic and abuse extremely well.

Ceramic floor tiles fall into one of two categories: vitreous ceramic mosaic or quarry. The first (VC) is made in two general types—clay and porcelain. Neither type has a baked-on glaze, but the tile material is colored throughout. As a result, any wearing of the surface leaves no change in the overall color of the tile.

Fig. 4-1. A ceramic tile floor—in a living room.

The clay type of vitreous tile is made from a fine, dense clay and is fired at a high temperature. High-temperature firing produces a tile that will hardly absorb any water. This low-moisture absorption makes clay tile ideal for either interior or exterior floors. Sometimes earth dyes or colors are added to the clay at the time of processing. Modern manufacturing processes can produce a tile with a veined or mottled color in addition to solid colors. These tiles are commonly produced in sizes of 1 inch square and are usually referred to as mosaic floor tile (Fig. 4-2). Mosaic tile has always been a favorite floor covering in bathrooms.

The porcelain type of vitreous ceramic mosaic floor tile is a denser formulation; it has purer color and slightly greater durability than clay tiles. Porcelain tile is made in sizes up to 2 inches square.

All VC floor tile comes in sheets, usually 2 feet square. The tile has a backing of either wide-mesh cloth or paper (called back-mounted tile). Another type of mosaic tile sheet is face mounted with paper. The latest development in sheet mosaic tile comes from the American Olean Tile Company: pregrouted tile sheets. With all three types of sheets, the floor is first covered with adhesive, then the tile is pressed into position. The back-mounted sheets must be grouted after the tile has set. The face-mounted sheets must also be grouted but first the face sheet must be removed. The pregrouted sheets produced by American Olean require only grouting between the sheets and are therefore much easier for first time users to work with.

The second category of ceramic floor tile is commonly referred to as quarry tile (Fig. 4-3). The name *quarry tile* does not mean that the tile is cut in a quarry from stone. Quarry tiles are fired in a kiln or large oven, just like other ceramic tile.

Quarry tiles are made in larger, thicker pieces than the VC floor tile; they are also denser and stronger. Because of their thickness (at least 1/2 inch), they stand up well to heavy traffic and heavy loads. Quarry tile is made from reddish-brown earth clay and occasionally with some color added.

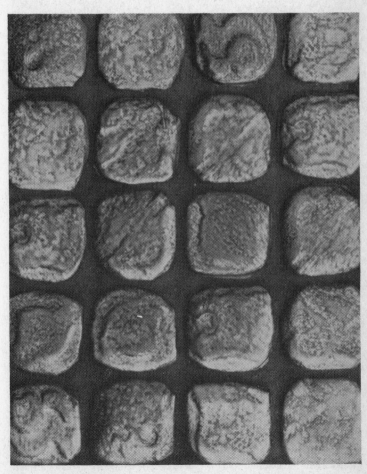

Fig. 4-2. Mosaic floor tiles.

Fig. 4-3. Quarry tile.

Quarry tile, as with all ceramic tile, has a very low water absorbency and a high resistance to abrasion. The tough, smooth surface will not retain odors, grease, dirt, acid, or moisture. These characteristics make quarry tile ideal for any area that is subject to abuse.

Generally speaking, the thicker the tile, the greater its ability to withstand heavy traffic and abuse. VC tile is usually 1/4 inch thick. Paver tile, a type of quarry tile, is usually 1/2 inch thick and can be obtained in the same variety of colors and designs as VC tile. Packinghouse tile is another kind of quarry tile; it's probably the toughest of all tiles. However, it usually comes in only a brownish red.

Glazed tile is another kind of quarry tile. Generally, the use of glazed tile is limited to walls because traffic will scratch, score, or crack the surface glaze should these tiles be used on heavy-traffic floors. However, glazed tile can be used for flooring where the traffic is light, areas such as dressing rooms, shower floors, or the hearth in front of a fireplace (Fig. 4-4).

TOOLS AND MATERIALS

Your local tile dealer is probably best qualified to estimate the number of tiles you'll need to cover a floor. But you have to help him

Fig. 4-4. Glazed ceramic tile.

out by drawing a sketch of the floor area, complete with relevant dimensions. Show him your sketch; he can use it to calculate the exact number of tiles you'll need.

Depending on the type of tile you buy, you will also need adhesive, grout, caulking (for around bathroom fixtures), denatured alcohol, and cheesecloth. The same dealer that sells you the tile can also recommend the best type of adhesive, grout, and caulking. You should use the materials that the tile manufacturer recommends.

The tools you will need for most tile installation jobs are as follows:

Chalk line
Notched trowel
Ruler
Caulking gun
Tile cutter or *carbide-tipped tile nippers*
150 pound roller—rented from tile dealer
Sandpaper and possibly a *belt sander*
Utility knife
Sponge
Level

SURFACE PREPARATION

Ceramic tile is heavier than any other type of floor covering, so the first step of surface preparation is to make sure the floor is solid. If the existing floor is springy, you must first cover it with 1/2-inch exterior grade waterproof plywood. If flooring joists need reinforcing, do this by nailing an extra joist alongside existing joists.

Floors should also be level. Check the floor with a level. Low spots in the center of the floor can usually be corrected by additional bracing to the flooring joists. If the floor has a perceptible sag, it may be necessary to brace up the existing joists with either screw jacks or double 2 × 4 studs at each end.

New concrete floors must be properly cured and dried before covering with ceramic tile. A simple test for dryness involves laying a 2-foot-square sheet of clear plastic on the surface of the floor. Weight the corners of the plastic with pieces of scrap lumber and let the plastic lie undisturbed for 24 hours. If water condenses on the floor or on the back of the sheet of plastic, the floor requires more drying time.

For good adhesion, the floor must be free of dirt, curing and hardening compounds, oil, and rough spots. Rough areas should be ground with a machine until sufficiently smooth or filled with a good quality underlayment cement.

Old concrete, terrazzo, or masonry floors should be cleaned thoroughly so the surface is free from scale, dust, dirt, paint, wax, oil, grease, or any other substance which might interfere with the holding power of the adhesive. Surface preparation, in this case, could entail grinding, sanding, or wire brushing to remove the unwanted surface coverings.

Wood floors are the most common type of floor in American homes, and they usually pose little problem to the home remodeler. Before laying ceramic tile on a wood floor, it's usually best to cover the floor with exterior plywood or underlayment board. You can use 1/4-inch underlayment board if the top floor layer consists of boards no wider than 3 inches. However, if the floorboards are over 3 inches wide, they should be face nailed first and then covered with 1/2-inch or heavier exterior plywood. Nail plywood or underlayment boards at 4-inch intervals with resin-coated or ring-shanked nails. Nails should be long enough to pass through the plywood or underlayment boards and about 1 inch into the flooring underneath. Countersink all nailheads.

Usually, single plywood subfloors of 5/8 or 3/4 inch thickness are suitable as a base for ceramic tile—if the flooring joists are spaced 16 inches on-center. Surface irregularities such as high spots, indentations, and gouges should be filled or sanded as needed to produce a flat surface.

If plywood subfloors or underlayment boards are used as a base for the tile, they should be primed with an oil base primer. Special attention should be given to the edges of the sheets to insure that they are sealed with the primer. Apply the primer with a brush for small areas and with a roller for large rooms. In some cases, priming won't be necessary if a skim coat of adhesive is first applied to the wood. The main reason for priming or extra adhesive is to make sure that the floor will be waterproof.

Old resilient flooring such as linoleum, cork, rubber, sheet vinyl, vinyl-asbestos, or asphalt tile all make suitable underlayment, providing they are structurally sound, smooth, dry, and clean. Badly worn spots should be leveled with a good quality underlayment cement. Holes and gouges should be treated in the same manner. Missing or broken resilient flooring tile should be either replaced with new pieces or filled with the same underlayment cement. Light sanding is usually necessary for all types of old resilient flooring to assure good adhesion.

Fig. 4-5. Laying pregrouted tile.

LAYING CERAMIC TILE

Years ago the only way to lay ceramic tile was in a bed of concrete. First a strong solid subfloor had to be constructed to hold up the enormous weight. Then reinforcing wire was laid on the floor, and then another coat of cement. When this dried, the adhesive coat was applied, on top of which the tile was laid. After the tile had set, the floor was grouted. Old tile floors like this are common in older homes; they seem to last forever. This old method of laying ceramic tile, called the mortar-bed method, is still used today, but it is really beyond the scope of this book because it requires a thorough knowledge of cement. Fortunately, complete satisfactory results can be quickly achieved with more modern methods.

Now almost anyone can set tile. Usually, the job involves applying adhesive to the surface of the floor, setting the tile into this adhesive, then grouting the spaces between the tiles to make the floor waterproof. Some tile now is available in pregrouted sheets, and this means that the job of setting tile is easier than ever. Only the joints between the sheets require grouting (Fig. 4-5).

Laying ceramic tile is not very different from laying nonceramic tile. First the room should be divided into four equal sections, as explained in Chapter 2.

Next, lay several sheets of tile along one chalk line, starting at the center point. Then lay several sheets of tile along the other chalk line (Fig. 4-6). Of course, the two chalk lines must be perpendicular to each other. After you are certain of this, continue to lay the sheets of tile until you reach a wall. Readjust the chalk lines so the sheets against the walls can be cut along a grout line. It may be necessary to adjust the chalk lines so the seams in the subfloor are at least 3 inches from any joints between the tile sheets. If you have to adjust the chalk lines, insure that they are perpendicular to each other by laying tile along the lines and making sure the lines just touch the tile sheets.

After you have laid the sheets of tile up to the wall and adjusted the starting lines, you can remove the tile and begin applying the adhesive. Start at the intersection of the chalk lines and spread the adhesive over one-quarter of the room or over an area that you can cover with tile in one hour or less (Fig. 4-7). Use the proper size notched trowel to spread the adhesive uniformly. But, do not spread adhesive over those areas where it will be necessary to cut tile to fit: at the wall-floor junction or around fixtures, for example. This will be done after the full-size sheets have been set into places.

Lay the first sheet of tile squarely on the intersecting chalk lines. Butt each sheet of tile against the edge(s) of the already laid sheets. Then roll the sheet down into place, keeping the butted edges tightly pressed together. It is important that you do not *slide* the sheets into place. Sliding causes the adhesive to ooze up through the joints, making them visible when the floor is completed.

If excess adhesive is forced up between the joints of the tile sheets, stop laying the tile and retrowel the adhesive. When properly applied, most adhesives will give you solid bonding with no excess.

Before cutting any sheets of tile, finish laying the full sheets. (Do not lay the sheets nearest the wall with adhesive until you've cut

Fig. 4-6. Lay the tile sheets along the chalk lines.

and fitted them properly.) Next, fit those sheets that require cutting *at the grout line*. Butt these sheets of tile firmly against the wall to determine which grout line should be cut. Cut the sheets with a utility knife or bend and snap them along the grout line (Fig. 4-8).

When laying a sheet against the wall, the edges should fall into place with very slight pressure. Place one edge of the sheet into the adhesive, then roll the rest of the sheet into position (Fig. 4-9). If fullness does occur, causing a buckle in the sheet, remove the fullness by trimming the sheet along the wall edge.

If you have to cut a tile sheet *between grout lines* for proper fitting against a wall, you will have to use a tile cutter (Fig. 4-10). First lay a full sheet over the space between the wall and the last sheet, butting it snugly against the wall. Use this overlaid sheet as a straightedge to draw a line on the sheet beneath it. Cut the sheet on the line with a tile cutter (rented from the tile dealer). Spread adhesive and lay the full sheet between the cut sheet and the wall.

Contour cuts for fitting tile sheets around pipes and fixtures can be made with a pair of carbide-tipped tile nippers (Fig. 4-11). First,

Fig. 4-7. Spread adhesive over one quarter of the floor.

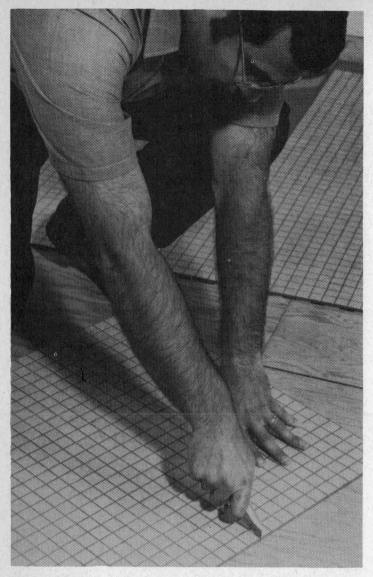

Fig. 4-8. Cut the tile sheets along the grout lines with a utility knife.

with a soft pencil, draw an approximate cut line on the face of the tile sheet. Remove whole tiles with a utility knife and then cut to the line with the tile nippers. Check the sheet for fit and remove additional bits of tile until you have an accurate fit. Spread adhesive and set the tile in the same manner as outlined above.

After the entire floor has been covered with tile, you should roll it with a 150-pound carpet-covered roller. To insure good adhesive contact, roll the floor in two directions with the roller. You should, however, wait at least 1 hour after installing the tile before rolling. In corners and other parts of the room where the roller cannot be used,

Fig. 4-9. Slip one edge of the tile sheet into place; roll the rest of the sheet down.

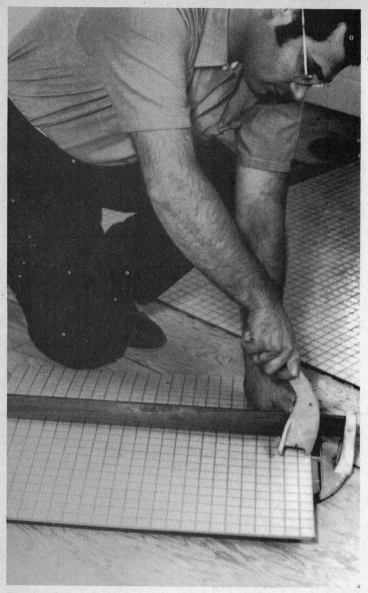

Fig. 4-10. Using a tile cutter.

place a piece of carpet-covered board over the area and pound with a hammer or mallet.

When the floor has been rolled and you are reasonably certain of a strong bond, you can apply caulking sealant around the edges of the room, around fixtures, and between the pregrouted sheets. (Tile sheets that aren't pregrouted will be discussed later.) The simplest way to caulk the edges around pregrouted sheets is with a tube of matching grout in a caulking gun. A 1/8-inch bead of caulking along

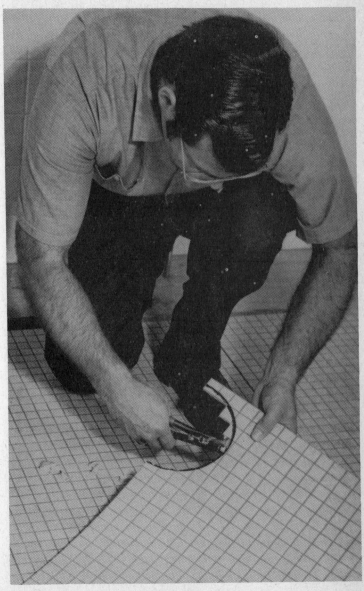

Fig. 4-11. Using carbide-tipped tile nippers.

the joint at the wall will give you a moisture seal and an attractive finished appearance. All plumbing fixtures, fittings, and spaces between the pregrouted sheets must also be sealed with the caulking.

Excess adhesive and caulking can be easily removed with a piece of cheese cloth dampened with denatured alcohol. Most tile manufacturers recommend that cleanup of adhesive and sealant should be done within 8 hours after installation. After this initial cleanup, washing with soap and water will maintain the original bright appearance of the floor.

GROUTING

If you install tile sheets that aren't grouted, it will be necessary to finish the job by grouting. There are several types of grout available: dry powders that require mixing, premixed grout that is applied directly from the can, and cartridges of grout that are used in a caulking gun (one example is Dow Corning's 784 Silicone Rubber Sealant). As with tile adhesives, it is best to use the type of grout recommended by the tile manufacturer. Follow the directions that come with the grout; this will insure predictable results.

Grout should not be applied to the joints of the tile until the adhesive has set for 24 to 36 hours. This will allow the adhesive to cure properly.

Apply the premixed or dry grout with a brush or sponge to all the joints. You can use a squeegee to compact grout in the joints. Allow the grout to set for a few minutes, then remove the excess from the face of the tiles as you further compact the grout into the joints. You should wear rubber gloves when working with grout; this will enable you to run a finger down the joints between the tile to insure uniformity. You might find it helpful to use the handle of a toothbrush to compact the grout.

After the grout begins to set, you can begin cleaning the faces of the tile. Do this with a damp sponge. Rinse the sponge often in clear, clean water, being careful not to disturb the grout in the joints. The trick is to use a damp, not wet, sponge.

You should caulk the joints around bathroom fixtures and where the floor meets the wall. Use a good quality silicone caulking for these areas.

After you wipe the surface of the tile with the clean damp sponge, let the floor dry and set overnight. The next day, after the grout has hardened, you can clean the face of the tile with a damp sponge. Then polish the tile with a clean soft rag. The job is finished at this point, but the floor should not be used for about 3 days. Cover the floor with polyethylene sheets and allow the floor to cure. If you need to use the room sooner, cover the polyethylene with plywood. After 3 days remove the covering and wash the floor with warm water and a sponge; then the floor may be used.

Your new tile floor will last for years with little or no maintenance. Because of the low absorption rate of ceramic tile, liquids will lie on the surface. You should, of course, wipe up any spills as soon as possible. During periodic cleaning you should be on the lookout for loose grout, which should be replaced as soon as possible.

If a tile should become damaged, it must be replaced as soon as possible. Begin repairs by removing all bits and pieces of the broken tile. It may be necessary to use a cold chisel and hammer to remove the tile. But if you use these tools, work carefully so as not to damage any of the neighboring tiles. Scrape or sand off the old adhesive. Determine what caused the tile to break and correct the problem.

After the space has been cleaned, apply new adhesive to the back of the replacement tile and set it into place. Press the new tile firmly into place and center it so the spacing around the tile is uniform. After at least 24 hours, the adhesive should be set enough so you can apply new grout around the tile.

The hardest part of replacing a broken tile is matching the new tile with tiles that have been in use for years. If you are installing a new tile floor, buy extra tiles and store them carefully. Unless you get matching tile at the time of installation, the chances of making a good match years later are slim. Manufacturers continually change colors and patterns, so matching can be very difficult.

Aside from the replacement of broken tile and periodic restoration of grout, a ceramic tile floor should outlast the installer. Occasional mopping may be necessary to restore the surface to like-new condition.

Chapter 5
Wood Floors

Wood is, by far, the most common type of interior floor covering in American homes. The availability, cost, ease of installation, and natural beauty of wood make it a superior choice for residential installation. Wood floors wear well in the home, and the inherent beauty enhances almost any decor.

THE FACTS ABOUT WOOD FLOORS

Wood floors are available in strip, plank, block, and tile form. Thicknesses range from the most common 25/32 to 53/32 inch. The thicker flooring should only be used where extra heavy-duty floors are required.

Wood floors are available in both hardwood and softwood. The most common types of hardwood floors are red and white oak, beech, birch, maple, and pecan. Softwoods most commonly used for flooring are southern pine, Douglas-fir, redwood, and western hemlock.

Softwood finish flooring costs less than most hardwood species and is often used to good advantage in bedroom and closet areas where traffic is light. It might also be selected to fit certain types of interior decors. Softwood finish flooring is less dense than the hardwoods, less wear resistant, and shows abrasions more readily. Softwood finish flooring is also less expensive than hardwood finish flooring.

In the older colonial homes in the Northeast, hardwood plank flooring is quite common. I have seen several homes, which were built in the early 1800s, that have wide (18 to 24 inches) maple plant floors. These floors were installed when wide planks were plentiful and very inexpensive. Now, it seems that only the wealthy can afford such floors. The rest of us must be content with standard 2 1/4-inch-wide strip flooring.

The most widely used type of finish flooring is 25/32- by 2 1/4-inch strip flooring. These strips are laid lengthwise in a room and normally at right angles to the floor joists. Strip flooring is, in most cases, tongued and grooved and end-matched (Fig. 5-1). Strips are random length and may vary from 2 to 16 feet or more. End-matched strip flooring in 25/32-inch thickness is generally hollow backed (Fig. 5-1A). The face of this type of flooring is wider than the back so tight joints result when the flooring is laid. The tongue fits tightly into the groove to prevent movement and floor squeaks. All of these minor details go a long way in helping to provide a finished floor that requires little or no maintenance.

Square-edged strip flooring is also available and is sometimes used in areas where appearance is not such an important factor (Fig. 5-1C). Square-edged strip flooring is less expensive than tongue-and-groove flooring because, obviously, fewer steps are required to produce it. Square-edged strip flooring must be face nailed to the subfloor and is therefore not as attractive as tongue-and-groove

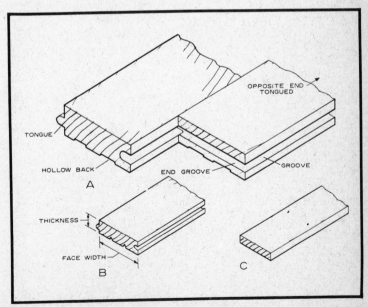

Fig. 5-1. Types of strip flooring.

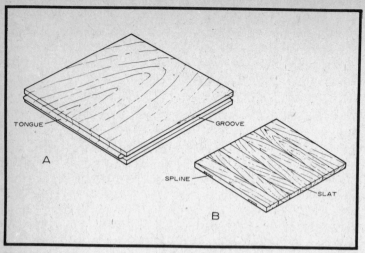

Fig. 5-2. Wood block flooring: A, tongue-and-groove; B, square-edged (splined).

flooring, which is blind nailed. The joints between square-edged strips are never as tight as those between tongue-and-groove strips. However, even with all its drawbacks, square-edged strip flooring is widely used in residential construction.

Another type of wood finish flooring is wood block flooring. Blocks may vary in size from 4 by 4 inches to 9 by 9 inches and larger. Thickness varies from 25/32 inch for laminated blocking or plywood block tile to 1/8 inch for stabilized veneer. Solid wood tile is often made up of narrow strips of wood splined or keyed together in a number of ways (Fig. 5-2B). Edges of the thicker tile are tongue and grooved (Fig. 5-2A), but thinner sections of wood are usually square edged. Plywood blocks may be 3/8 inch thick or more and are usually tongue and grooved. Many block floors are factory finished and require only waxing after installation. One very popular type of wood block flooring installation is the parquet style; the grains of the blocks are laid perpendicular to each other, in a kind of checkered pattern. Wood block flooring, depending on thickness, can be blind nailed or glued to the subfloor.

Prefinished solid wood block, prefinished veneer block, and prefinished strip flooring are becoming more popular than ever with home remodelers, and the flooring industry is increasing production to meet demand. Generally speaking, prefinished flooring costs more initially than conventional flooring. But in the long run, prefinished flooring is competitive in price. Installation of prefinished flooring is most often done with adhesive, and the results are compatible with finish flooring that is installed in the conventional manner (nailing).

SURFACE PREPARATION
AND INSTALLATION PROBLEMS

Before any type of finish flooring can be installed, the existing floor or subfloor must be checked thoroughly to insure that the surface is sound and level.

An important point to consider when installing new finish flooring over an existing finish floor is that the new floor will be higher. The height of the new finish floor will, of course, depend on the thickness of the new flooring and underlayment. As mentioned earlier, finish flooring can be as thick as 25/32 inch. Usually, the thickness of the new flooring will pose few problems, but sometimes there will be more work. Door jambs and doors may have to be tailored to the new floor height. This usually means that the door bottoms will have to be cut. You may also have to install door sills in doorways if the flooring is installed only in one room.

Heating systems, whether baseboard or hot air floor registers, will in most cases also have to be raised to compensate for the new floor height. If you have hot water baseboard heating, the amount of work involved may be beyond your ability. If so, you should consider having a qualified plumber or heating system worker do this part of the renovation. Hot air floor registers are much easier to raise and, in fact, can usually be raised with a sheet metal collar sold specifically for this purpose.

If you have a fireplace with the hearth on the floor, you may have a real problem. Generally speaking, you will have to end the new flooring around the hearth and finish off the job with some type of molding, if possible. It may be necessary to use slate or firebrick to finish the new flooring installation. Raised hearth fireplaces usually do not present any problems; however, you may have some difficulty cutting the last strip or block to fit into the contours of the brick or stone.

TOOLS AND MATERIALS

Estimating the amount of wood floor covering you'll need is usually fairly easy. Begin by measuring the perimeter of the room (or rooms), taking into consideration alcoves, closets, permanent fixtures, and cabinets. Determine, if you are using strip flooring, which direction the flooring will run. It is common practice to run strip flooring at right angles to the floor joists. In a conventionally designed house, the floor joists span the width of the building across a center supporting beam or wall. Thus, the finish flooring of the entire floor area of a rectangular house will be laid in the same direction. Flooring with L- or T-shaped plans will usually have a direction change at the wings, depending on joist direction. Since joists usually span lengthwise to the room. This will reduce shrinkage and swelling of the floor during seasonal changes.

Since block flooring is usually installed with adhesive, you do not have to concern yourself with joist direction.

When ordering tongue-and-groove strip flooring, you must order an additional 30%, to make up for the loss of coverage due to the tongue-and-groove milling.

Various types of nails are used in nailing different thicknesses of flooring. For 25/32-inch flooring, you may use eightpenny flooring nails; for 1/2-inch flooring, sixpenny nails; and for 3/8-inch flooring, fourpenny casing (finishing) nails. Since most square-edged or unmilled strip flooring is thinner than tongue-and-groove strip flooring, the nails most commonly used to face nail are 1 1/2-inch brads.

One type of nail used more frequently by professional builders is worth mentioning here. The annular-shanked, or threaded, nail is the nail of choice for face nailing square-edged and tongue-and-groove flooring. These nails have greater holding power than conventional plain-shanked nails. For example, a plain-shanked nail has a holding power of approximately 90 pounds, but a properly threaded nail of the same size will provide as much as 10 times the holding power. This means that smaller or fewer threaded flooring nails can be used to attach finish flooring. Slender threaded nails are at least one gauge smaller in diameter than common wire nails. This means that the threaded nails can be driven faster and with less chance of splitting the flooring.

A hammer isn't the only tool used to nail down wood flooring. Tongue-and-groove strip finish flooring can be nailed down with a manually operated floor nailing machine. You can usually rent one of these machines from the flooring supplier or from a tool rental shop. The floor nailing machine uses special nails that are joined into clips 2 inches long. The head of one of these special nails is at a right angle to the shank. This kind of nail resembles an inverted L.

To operate the floor nailing machine, simply load clips of nails into a slot and position the machine on the tongue of the strip flooring. Next, strike a mallet against a cap on top of the machine. This action drives a nail, at an angle, through the tongue of the flooring and into the subfloor. The head of the nail is driven flush with the tongue and will be hidden by the next piece of flooring. The floor nailing machine is an incredible time saver, and it is easy to use. After you become familiar with its operation, you will develop a rhythm of placing the machine into position, striking with the mallet, and repositioning and striking again until the piece of flooring is securely fastened to the subfloor. The floor nailing machine can be used to attach all the tongue-and-groove finish flooring except the first three courses (or rows) parallel to a wall. These must be nailed by hand.

Flooring should be delivered to the building site at least three days before installation is to begin. This will give the flooring enough time to become acclimated to the temperature and moisture of the house. The house temperature is important, and the flooring should be stored at temperatures ranging from 50° to 70°F. Moisture content of the house should also be low or the flooring will absorb moisture before installation. Moisture absorbed after delivery to the house site is one of the most common causes of open joints between flooring strips that appear after several months of the heating season.

INSTALLING WOOD STRIP FLOORING

Board and plywood subfloors should be clean, level, and covered with heavy building or tar paper. This paper will stop a certain amount of dust, will help to deaden sound, and will help to increase the warmth of the floor by preventing air and moisture infiltration. To add increased insulation, some builders in the northern sections of the country, in addition to the tar paper, also use aluminum foil (designed for the purpose). Some builders claim that the reflective qualities of this foil help to keep heat in the room and the cold out.

To make nailing of the flooring to the joists easier, you should mark the location of the joists. This can be easily done by striking chalk lines across the entire room, over the flooring paper. A much better job results when you nail the finish floor, the subfloor, and the joists together. But this isn't always possible.

Tongue-and-Groove Strip Flooring

After the flooring paper has been laid over the floor and the location of the joists is marked with chalk lines, you can begin installing the first row of tongue-and-groove strip flooring. The first strip is attached parallel to the wall and spaced 1/2 to 5/8 inch from the wall. This space allows for expansion of the strips when the moisture content of the room increases. The first strip is usually face nailed 1/2 inch from the grooved edge of the strip. These nails

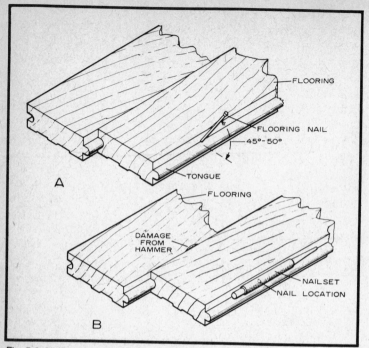

Fig. 5-3. Nailing the tongue at an angle (A); setting the nail with a nailset (B).

should be driven into the joist and as near the wall edge of the strip as possible. These face nails can later be covered by baseboard or shoe moldings.

The first strip can also be nailed through the tongue at an angle of 45°, into the joist below (Fig. 5-3A). At this point, the nail should not be driven flush with the strip or you may damage the edge of the strip. Later the nail can be set (slightly countersunk) with a large nailset or by pressing the nailset flat against the nail (Fig. 5-3B). If you are using a nailing machine, the nail will be driven into the flooring and set all in one shot with a single blow of the mallet.

If I am installing hardwood flooring, such as oak, I find it necessary to drill holes through the flooring before face nailing. Oak flooring is much too hard to nail through without such holes. Also there is less chance of splitting the flooring if nail holes are first drilled. These nail holes should be approximately 1/2 inch from the grooved edge and spaced around 16 inches on-center (if the joists are 16 inches center-to-center).

After the first strip, or series of strips, have been installed parallel to the wall, the second series of strips can be attached. Butt the second strip against the first and tap lightly with a rubber mallet to insure a tight joint. A rubber mallet is used because it will not damage the edge of the strips. The joints must be tight along the entire length of the strips, and in most cases some tapping of the mallet will persuade the strip into position.

It is important, for the second and later courses of flooring, to select pieces that are either longer or shorter than pieces in the first course. The idea is to have joints that are well separated. For example, if you start the first course with a strip that is 6 feet long, start the second course with a strip that is 4 feet long.

The work will go quicker if one person nails the flooring while another lays out the strips in courses. The helper should try to minimize waste and make sure the joints are staggered. He should also select the straightest pieces of finish flooring; this will minimize the amount of work involved.

Each course (after the first) of strip flooring is nailed in the same way: through the tongue. It may be necessary at the ends of strips to predrill the nail holes. This will reduce the chances of splitting the strip.

The last course of flooring may have to be cut lengthwise so it will fit between the wall and the rest of the finish flooring. It is common practice, as with the first course, to leave a 1/2- to 5/8-inch space between the wall and the last flooring strip. The last strip is also face nailed so the baseboard or shoe molding covers the set nailheads.

If you are installing strip finish flooring throughout an entire house, you should do all the rooms first, then the doorways. After all the rooms have been completed, you can continue out into the hallway.

Square-Edged Strip Flooring

Installation of square-edged strip flooring is similar to the installation of tongue-and-groove strip flooring except that the joints between the strips are not interlocked. Also, since there are no tongues through which to nail, square-edged strip flooring must be face nailed or attached with screws and wooden plugs (in the strip face).

Square-edged strip flooring is available in widths from 4 inches to 18 inches, with 8-inch widths being the most common. Strip flooring in the wider widths is often called plank flooring. One problem that all wide strip flooring has in common is cupping; that is, dishing upward after installation. The only way that cupping can be prevented is to securely fasten the planks to the subfloor and joists.

Face nailing square-edged strips is the fastest method of securing the planks to the subfloor. Usually, nails should be driven through the planks on 16-inch centers and ideally into the flooring joists below. Nails are driven in pairs in strips up to 8 inches wide, and a minimum of three nails for the wider planks. Nails should be either ring shanked or threaded and should be made from aluminum in order to avoid rusting when the floor is later cleaned. Though face nailing is the quickest method of attaching these planks, it is not the most attractive, for the nail heads are always visible. I would recommend that you only face nail planks made from pine or fir.

Hardwood plank flooring is costly but quite beautiful if installed properly. The most attractive method of attachment is by screwing the boards down and then covering the countersunk screwheads with wooden plugs. First, the plank is positioned as tightly as possible against the previously laid plank. It may be necessary to use some type of wedging affair to hold the plank in position while it is drilled and screwed into place. The screws must be countersunk deep enough so a wooden plug can be fitted on top.

When the entire floor has been laid, with all the screws countersunk, you can go back and fit the holes with wooden plugs. Wooden plugs can be of the same variety wood or of another type for contrast. Put a drop or two of white glue into each hole before fitting the plug. Wooden plugs should be slightly wider than the hole and, if necessary, tapered on the end that will be inserted into the hole. The plug should also be longer than the hole is deep. Later, when the floor is sanded, before finishing, the excess plug can be ground down flush with the floor.

Fastening wide strip flooring with screws and then filling the holes with wooden plugs will take more time than you can imagine. But the look of a hardwood plank floor with wooden plugs throughout is most unusual and, I think, worth the extra effort involved.

INSTALLING BLOCK AND TILE WOOD FLOORING

Block and tile are two other types of wood flooring that are common in American homes. In most cases both of these types are installed with adhesive on a plywood subfloor base. The exception is the 25/32-inch wood blocks, which have tongues on two edges and grooves on the other two edges. If the subfloor is plywood or other conventional flooring, these blocks are commonly nailed through the tongue into the base. However, if the subfloor is concrete, adhesive must be used to attach the blocks. Wood block flooring is installed with the grain direction changed on alternating blocks. By changing the grain direction on every other block you minimize the chances of shrinkage and swelling of the wood.

One type of wood floor tile is made up of a number of narrow slats that form a 4- × 4-inch square. Four or more of these squares, with alternating grain direction, form a block. The slats, squares, and blocks are held together with a removable membrane. Adhesive is spread on the concrete slab, subfloor, or underlayment with a notched trowel, and the blocks are installed immediately. The membrane is then removed and the blocks are tamped into place for full adhesive contact. A conventional floor tile roller can also be used for added pressure. Manufacturer's directions for adhesive, trowel tooth depth, and method of installation must always be followed. Similar tile made up of narrow strips of wood are fastened together with small rabbeted cleats, tape, or similar fastening. They too are normally applied with adhesive in accordance with the manufacturer's recommendations.

Most wood block and tile is prefinished at the factory. Therefore, once the installation has been completed and the adhesive is set up for the required time, the floor is finished.

FINISHING WOOD FLOORS

Most strip and plank floors will require sanding and two or more coats of a protective coating before the job is completed.

Interior wood floor finishing begins with sanding, usually with a rented floor sander designed for this purpose. Sanding is desirable because it will remove the variations in height that often occur between strip flooring. A newly laid floor is sanded in three operations. The first pass is made *at right angles* to the strip flooring, using a coarse close-coated sandpaper. The second pass, of the sanding machine, is made *with* the grain (parallel), using medium-close grit sandpaper. The third and final pass is also made parallel to the grain, using a fine-grit sandpaper. After the third pass of the sander, the surface of the floor should be smooth and flat all over.

A conventional floor sander has a few limitations that you will become aware of as you use it. Floor sanders cannot sand close to walls or in corners. The area that lies next to a wall must be done with either an edger or by hand. If you have one or more rooms or long walls, you will have your work cut out for you if you do this area by hand. An edger sands in a circular motion and has wheels on its base that help move it along the floor, at the wall-floor junction.

Corners are sanded by hand using a special tool called a corner, or hook, scraper. The blade of this tool is placed in the corner and pressure is applied with one hand while the other hand pulls the tool towards the user. The blade will dull rather quickly, so you should have a flat file handy to resharpen the tool.

Floor sanders do a very effective and efficient job of sanding a floor, but there are a few cautions you should be aware of. First, keep the machine moving at all times while the sandpaper drum is turning. Some floor sanders operate on 220 volts, so make sure you have a suitable hookup for the sander (kitchen range, air conditioner, or temporary hookup). While operating the sander it is advisable to drape the excess cord over your shoulder and down your back to keep it away from the work area. A floor sander can sever the cord before you know what's happening.

After the floor has been sanded it should be vacuumed thoroughly to remove the dust created by the sanding process. Then you must decide what type of finish you want on the floor. Finishes may be *glossy* or *flat*. You may want to stain the floor with a penetrating stain or finish with a clear coating to let the natural beauty of the wood show through.

A filler is required for wood with large pores, such as oak or walnut, if a smooth, glossy finish is desired. A filler may be paste or liquid, clear or colored. Filler is usually first brushed on the floor *across* the grain and then *with* the grain. Surplus filler must be removed after most of the floor has dried. Then the filler coat should be allowed to dry thoroughly before the finish coats are applied.

Stains are sometimes used to obtain a more nearly uniform color when individual boards vary too much in their natural color. Stains may also be used to accent the grain of the floor. Oil-base penetrating stains should be applied so that worn areas will blend in with the rest of the floor.

Finishes commonly used for wood floors are classified as either sealers or varnishes. Sealers, which are usually thinned out varnishes, are widely used in residential flooring. They penetrate the wood just enough to avoid formation of a surface coating of appreciable thickness. Wax is usually applied over the sealer for a low-luster finish. Wax floors, however, require periodic waxing to restore the finish, especially in high-traffic areas.

Varnish floors are glossy and generally require less maintenance than waxed floors. There are several types of varnishes available for floors, and some are more durable than others. Personally, I prefer to use polyurethane, for it is clear, wears like iron, and protects the natural beauty of the floor.

After the floor is sealed, if necessary, I apply a coat of polyurethane, using a roller with an extension handle. I start on the far side of the room by pouring a pint or so of the finish onto the floor. The polyurethane is then rolled out with the roller. I continue covering the floor in the same way, working my way out of the room as I go. I let the first coat dry for 24 hours before applying the second and final coat, again using a roller. Before the second coat is applied I remove the gloss by lightly going over the entire floor with steel wool.

Polyurethane's gloss will last for many years with no maintenance. It may be necessary, however, to recoat the floor with the same type of finish after 5 or 10 years, depending on the amount of traffic.

As I mentioned earlier, most block and tile flooring is prefinished at the factory, so the job is completed when the adhesive has dried.

Chapter 6
Floor Problems

Floors in most homes will develop some kind of problem at one time or another. Some of these problems may be readily apparent, such as squeaking floorboards, sagging, or springiness; other problems may be well concealed: mildew, dry rot, or termites. Still another type of problem is damage to the surface of the floor.

MOISTURE

Without a doubt, the greatest source of trouble to interior floors is moisture, which is mainly caused by condensation. In the colder regions of the United States, where the January temperatures average 35°F or lower, the first signs of spring may include dark stains on house siding and peeling paint. These often indicate a cold weather condensation problem.

Condensation can be described as the change in moisture from a vapor to a liquid. In homes not properly protected, condensation caused by high humidities often results in excessive maintenance costs. Estimates have been made that a typical family of four converts 3 gallons of water into water vapor per day. Unless excess water vapor is properly removed in some way (usually ventilation), it will either increase the humidity or condense on cold surfaces such as window glass. It can move through the house structure, often condensing *within* the wall, roof, or floor cavities. Heating systems equipped with winter air conditioning systems (humidifiers) will add moisture to the air.

Condensation will take place any time the temperature drops below the dew point. The dew point is the temperature at which vapor begins to condense. Water vapor cooled below the dew point appears in the atmosphere as fog and on the earth's surface as dew or frost. This means that water vapor will condense on surfaces that have a temperature below the dew point.

During cold weather, condensation is usually first noticed on window glass but may also be discovered on closet and unheated bedroom walls and ceilings. Another area where visible condensation can occur is in crawl spaces under occupied rooms. This area usually differs from those inside the house because the source of the moisture is usually from the soil or from warm moisture-laden air that enters through foundation ventilators. Vapor then condenses on the cooler during warm periods in late spring.

Ventilation used in proper amounts and locations is a recognized means of controlling condensation in buildings. Inlet and outlet ventilators in crawl spaces aid in preventing accumulation of condensation.

Crawl space moisture can be virtually eliminated by a vapor barrier over the soil. When such protection is used, the need for ventilation is usually reduced to only 10% of that required when a soil cover is not present. The control of condensation through the use of vapor barriers and ventilation should be practiced regardless of the amount of insulation used (Fig. 6-1).

A good rule of thumb to keep in mind when installing vapor barriers in a house is: Place the vapor barrier as close as possible to the interior, or warm, surface of all exterior walls, ceilings, and floors. This normally means placing the vapor barrier (separately or as a part of the insulation) between the subfloor and the finish floor. But there's an alternative method: If there's an unheated crawl space, you can put a barrier just under the subfloor—as long as you also put one directly on the soil. Insulation is, of course, fastened between the joists (Fig. 6-1). The exception is the insulation used with concrete floor slabs where a barrier is used under the insulation to protect it from ground moisture.

A house that is constructed on a concrete slab must be protected from soil moisture which may enter the slab. Protection is normally provided by a vapor barrier, which completely isolates the concrete and perimeter insulation from the soil. Thermal insulation of some type is required around the house perimeter in the colder climates, not only to reduce heat loss but also to minimize condensation on the colder surfaces. Some type of rigid insulation impervious

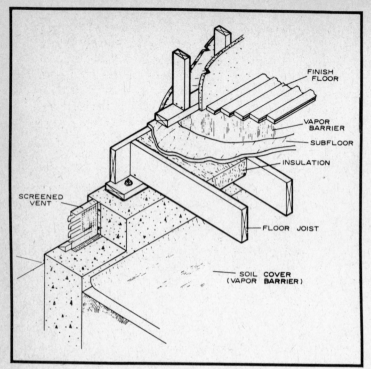

Fig. 6-1. Crawl space vent and vapor barrier.

to moisture should be used. Expanded plastic insulation such as polystyrene is commonly used.

In late spring or early summer, periods of high humidity may cause surface condensation on exposed concrete slabs or on floor coverings such as resilient tile. A full insulated slab or wood floor installed over wood furring strips minimizes or eliminates such problems.

In general, to provide complete protection from condensation, the conventional unheated crawl space should contain foundation ventilators, a vapor barrier, and thermal insulation between the floor joists. Foundation ventilators are normally located near the top of the masonry wall. In concrete block foundations, the ventilator is often made in a size that can easily substitute for a full concrete block.

The amount of ventilation required for a crawl space is based on the total area of the house and the presence of a vapor barrier soil cover. As pointed out earlier, less ventilation is required for an unheated crawl space that has a vapor barrier over the soil.

In placing the vapor barrier over the crawl space soil, edges should be folded slightly and the ends should be turned up on the foundation wall (Fig. 6-1). To prevent movement of the barrier, it is good practice to weight down folds and edges with bricks or stone.

When installing insulation between the floor joists, one rule must be observed: A vapor barrier must be either inserted between the subfloor and the finish floor or attached to the insulation.

One way to install between-the-joist insulation is to use mastic to adhere it to the subfloor above. This method works best on friction-type batt insulation (Fig. 6-2A). The insulation fits snugly between the joists and thus takes some of the weight off the mastic.

Floor insulation may also be supported by a wire mesh stretched between wood strips, as in Fig. 6-2B. This method is especially well adapted to insulation with an attached vapor barrier. Another method used to install insulation consists of using small wood strips sprung across the joist space (Fig. 6-2C). The strips are cut slightly longer than the width of the space and sprung in place so they press against the bottom of the insulation.

When only a small amount of insulation is required between the joists because of moderate climates, several other insulating materials can be used. One such material is reflective paper with aluminum foil on each face. The reflective face must be placed at least 3/4 inch away from the underside of the subfloor to be fully effective. Multiple or expanded reflective insulation might also be used. A thin blanket insulation can also be used between the joists. This is installed in much the same manner as thicker insulations. When vapor barriers are a part of the flexible insulation and properly installed, no additional vapor barrier is ordinarily required.

DECAY

Wood decay is caused by certain fungi that eat wood. These fungi, like other plants, require air, warmth, food, and moisture for growth. Early stages of decay caused by these fungi may be accompanied by a discoloration of the wood. Advanced decay is easily recognized because the wood has undergone definite changes in strength and appearance. In advanced stages of decay, the affected wood generally is brown and crumbly and sometimes may be comparatively white and spongy. These changes may not be apparent on the surface, but the loss of sound wood inside often is reflected by sunken areas on the surface or by a hollow sound when the wood is tapped with a hammer. Where the surrounding atmosphere is very damp, the fungi may grow out on the surface, appearing as white or brownish growths in patches or strands.

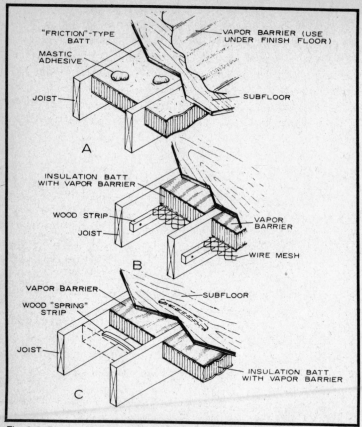

Fig. 6-2. Friction-type batts, A; wire mesh support, B; wood strip support, C.

Wood-destroying fungi will not become established in dry wood. A moisture content of 20% (which can be determined by an electrical moisture meter) is safe. Moisture contents greater than this are practically never reached in wood sheltered from rain and protected against wetting by ground moisture. Decay can be permanently arrested by simply taking measures to dry out the infected wood and to keep it dry. Brown crumbly decay, in the dry condition, is sometimes called *dry rot*.

The presence of mold or stain fungi should serve as a warning that conditions are or have been suitable for decay fungi. Heavily molded or stained lumber, therefore, should be examined for evidence of decay. If decayed or rotten floor joists are found, they should be replaced after the cause of the problem has been determined.

Fortunately there are a few safeguards that can be employed to insure that decay does not get a start in your house's crawl space. As mentioned earlier, the three best defenses against moisture are vapor barriers, ventilation, and thermal insulation. In addition you should never have any untreated wood in direct contact with the soil. The foundation walls should have a clearance of at least 8 inches above the exterior finish grade, and there should be a clearance of 18 inches or more from the bottom of the joists to the ground in crawl spaces.

TERMITES

Wood is subject to attack by termites and other insects. Termites can be grouped into two main classes: subterranean and dry-wood. Subterranean termites are mainly prevalent in northern states. Buildings may be fully protected against subterranean termites by incorporating comparatively inexpensive protection measures during construction. The Formosan subterranean termite was discovered in 1966 in several locations in the South. It is a serious pest. Though presently in localized areas, it could easily spread to other areas. Controls are similar to those for other subterranean species. Dry-wood termites are found principally in Florida, Southern California, and the Gulf Coast states. They are more difficult to control, but the damage is less serious than that caused by subterranean termites.

One of the requirements for subterranean termite life is moisture in the soil. These termites become most numerous in moist, warm soil containing an abundant supply of food in the form of wood or other cellulosic material. In their search for additional wood, they build earth-like shelter tubes on foundation walls or in cracks in the walls or on pipes or supports leading from the soil to the house. These tubes are usually from 1/4 to 1/2 inch wide; they are flattened and protect the termites in their travels between food and shelter.

Since subterranean termites eat the interior of the wood, they may cause much damage before they are discovered. They honeycomb the wood with tunnels separated by thin layers of sound wood.

Dry-wood termites fly directly to and bore into wood, instead of building tunnels from the ground as do the subterranean termites. Dry-wood termites are common in the tropics, and damage has been recorded in the United States in a narrow strip along the Atlantic Coast from Cape Henry, Virginia to the Florida Keys, westward along the Gulf Coast to as far as Northern California. Serious damage

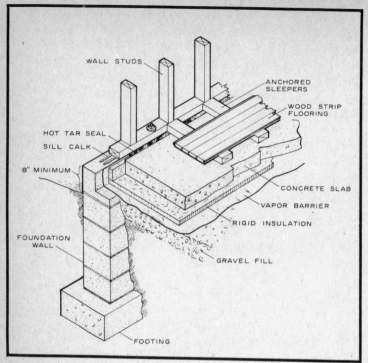

Fig. 6-3. No wood should touch the soil.

has been noted in Southern California and in localities around Tampa, Miami, and Key West.

The best time to provide protection against termites is during the planning and construction of the building. The first requirement is to remove all woody debris like stumps and discarded boards from the soil at the building site before and after construction. Steps should also be taken to keep the soil under the house as dry as possible.

Next, the foundation should be made impervious to subterranean termites to prevent them from crawling up through hidden cracks to the wood in the building above. Properly reinforced concrete makes the best foundation, but unit-construction walls or piers capped with at least 4 inches of reinforced concrete are also satisfactory. No wood member of the house should be in contact with the soil (Fig. 6-3).

The best protection against subterranean termites is by treating the soil near the foundation or under an entire slab foundation. The effective soil treatments are water emulsions of aldrin (0.5%), dieldrin (0.5%), or heptachlor (0.5%). The rate of application is 4 gallons per 10 linear feet at the edge and along expansion joints of slabs or along a foundation. For brick or hollow-block foundations, the rate is 4 gallons per 10 linear feet for each foot of depth to the footing. One to 1 1/2 gallons of emulsion per 10 square feet of surface area is recommended for overall treatment before pouring concrete slab foundations.

In regions where dry-wood termites thrive, all doors, windows (especially attic windows), and other ventilated openings should be screened (not less than 20 meshes to the inch). All cracks, crevices, and joints between exterior wood members should be filled with a mastic caulking or plastic wood. Several coats of house paint will provide considerable protection to exterior woodwork in buildings.

Pesticides used improperly can be injurious to man, animals, and plants. Follow the directions and heed all precautions on the labels.

AGING

As a house ages, the floor joists, subfloor, and finish flooring will usually become very dry. This dryness results in shrinkage and precipitates problems such as squeaking, sagging, springy floors, and drafts. In most cases these problems can be remedied quickly and easily.

Squeaks are usually caused by movement of one board against another. Such movement may occur because (1) floor joists are too light, causing excessive deflection, (2) sill plates over concrete slabs are not held down tightly, (3) tongues are loose, or (4) nailing is poor. Adequate nailing is an important means of minimizing squeaks, and another is to apply finish floors only after the joists have dried to a 12% moisture content or less. A much better job results when you nail the finish floor through the subfloor into the joists than if you nail the finish floor only to the subfloor.

One very quick remedy for a squeaking section of floor is to face nail the culprits. Although this will solve the problem, it is not esthetically pleasing to see nailheads on a finish floor, especially if the floor is hardwood. Another solution is to work from below the squeak, in the basement or crawl space. It will be necessary to have a helper stand on the squeaking area while you mark the location from beneath the floor. Then you can install some type of bridging between the joists (Fig. 6-4).

Sagging floors are usually the result of lumber shrinkage and are corrected from underneath. Sagging floors are an indication that the

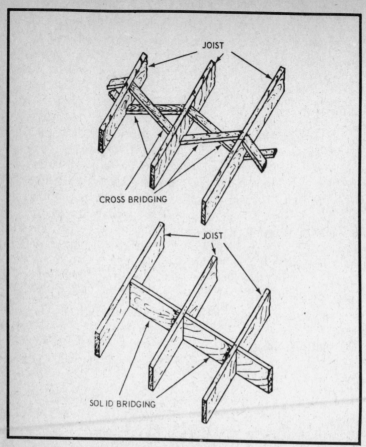

Fig. 6-4. Cross bridging and solid bridging.

joists are either not strong enough or they have shrunk slightly, causing the floor to sag. Another possible cause of sagging floors is a sagging girder. Girders are load-bearing structural members. They help support the floor joists. Girders are supported by posts, columns, or screw jacks. In most cases girders will not move. However, if a wooden support should become rotten or shrink more than normal, a girder will sag.

To correct a sagging girder, you must jack it back up into position (or slightly higher) and then install a new post. This is most easily accomplished by using a screw type jack. The jack can usually be rented from a lumberyard or tool rental shop.

Springy floors result when the joists are not strong enough to prevent deflection. The solution to this problem is to add extra joists, the same size as the existing ones. The extras are nailed directly to the existing joists.

SPECIAL PROBLEMS WITH STRIP FLOORING

In addition to the problems covered in the last section (squeaking, sagging, and springy floors), strip flooring sometimes develops some other common problems. The usual problems include broken or damaged strips, loose strips, cupping, and strip edge irregularities.

Strips become damaged when heavy objects are dropped on the floor, when heavy furniture rests for long periods without coasters, or when there is continual heavy traffic on the floor. Replacing damaged strip flooring (either tongue-and-groove or square-edged) requires only a few simple tools and a little time. If there is a great color difference between the new strips and the existing flooring, you may decide to refinish the entire floor after the repairs have been made.

Begin repairs by removing the damaged strip. This is most easily accomplished by using a hammer and wood chisel. Work slowly, splitting the damaged pieces out with the chisel, being careful that you don't damage the adjacent boards. After the damaged strip is removed and the area is cleaned, cut a new length of strip flooring the same size as the one just removed.

If the new strip is square edged, simply fit in place snugly—a hammer and scrap block may be helpful. Then face nail the new strip through the subfloor and into the joist below. If, however, the new replacement strip is tongue and grooved, you must remove the bottom half of the groove before installing. This will enable you to slide it in at an angle so the tongue edge meshes first. Tap the grooved side down with a hammer and scrap piece of block. Complete the repair by face nailing at the edges with case or finishing nails. If necessary, drill pilot holes for the nails.

If the existing floor was finished with stain or clear finish, you should try to match the finish on the new strip *before* installing or the repair will be apparent.

The best solution for loose strip flooring is to face nail the strip. Drill pilot holes first and countersink or set the nailhead.

Strip edge irregularities occur as a strip floor ages. This is also a sign of improper nailing of plank flooring and is, in that case, called cupping. There are two possible solutions, depending on the type of floor. For plank floors, it is usually best to face nail, providing you can live with exposed nailheads. If you can't, you should consider face nailing, countersinking the nailheads, and then fitting wooden plugs into the holes.

The other solution to strip edge irregularities is to sand the entire floor. Sanding, with a machine designed for the purpose, will make the surface of the floor flat, with all the edges of the strips even. The floor should, after the sanding, be refinished with either a clear finish or stain.

SPECIAL PROBLEMS WITH RESILIENT FLOORING

Resilient flooring includes nonceramic tile and sheet vinyl. There are relatively few problems associated with resilient flooring, and when these problems exist the solutions are usually simple. The most common problems are nailhead popping (from the subfloor up through the tile), indentations, damaged or worn tile, loose or curled edges, popping tiles, and loose perimeter on sheet vinyl flooring.

Nailhead popping occurs when the subfloor contains moisture before the tile is laid. As the subfloor dries, the nails work themselves up and become visible as bumps in the tile floor. The only solution is to go over the entire floor with a hammer and scrap piece of wood and tap the nails back into place. In most cases this will remedy the problem.

Indentations occur when the subfloor has dents or spaces. As resilient flooring ages it will settle into any recessed areas in the subfloor. One solution is to remove the tile (using a chisel or putty knife and hammer), fill the indentation in the subfloor with a filler such as a white glue and sawdust mixture, and then install a new tile.

Damaged or worn tiles can be removed with the same tools; the repair can be made in the same fashion.

Loose, curled edges usually result when either there has been excessive moisture in the floor or there hasn't been enough adhesive used in the initial installation. After the source of the trouble has been determined and dealt with, you should remove all the loose tiles. Clean out the area underneath the tile, apply new adhesive, and then reinstall a new tile.

Occasionally the edges of sheet vinyl flooring will come loose. This is usually a sign of improper installation. The best solution is to roll the sheet away from the wall, clean the subfloor, apply new adhesive, roll the flooring back into place, and weight it down until the adhesive sets. In special cases, where the sheet is stubborn, you can, in addition to applying new adhesive, face nail or staple close to the edge. Then you can add new moldings to cover the nailheads.

SPECIAL PROBLEMS WITH CERAMIC TILE

Problems with ceramic tile include damaged tile, loose or missing grout in the joints, or irregularities. Damaged tile is removed with a hammer and chisel. New adhesive is applied, and a replacement tile is installed. The major problem in repairing damaged tile is matching the old tile. Unless you have saved some ceramic tile from the initial installation, it is almost impossible to make a perfect match.

In time, the grout in the tile joints may become loose or deteriorate. Also, if an old tile is removed, the grout around that tile must also be removed. There are several ways to regrout a floor, but the easiest is to use a silicone caulking, available in tubes and applied with the aid of a caulking gun.

Chapter 7
Gypsum Ceilings

The least expensive, easiest to install, and most common interior ceiling covering in use in American homes is gypsum board, also called plasterboard and Sheetrock. For the sake of simplicity, I'll use the term Sheetrock (a trade name belonging to United States Gypsum).

THE FACTS ABOUT SHEETROCK

Sheetrock is made from calcined gypsum mixed with water and other ingredients to form a dense, hardened panel. The back side of the panel is covered with a strong liner paper, and the face is covered with a heavy manila finished paper.

Sheetrock panels are available in thicknesses of 1/4, 3/8, 1/2, and 5/8 inches and in even lengths of 6 to 14 feet. Standard width is 4 feet. The easiest size panel for the homeowner to work with is the common 4- by 8-foot panel, 1/2 inch thick. The weight of this standard size panel is around 2 pounds per square foot or approximately 60 pounds per panel.

In new construction, Sheetrock panels are most commonly attached directly to the ceiling joists. Panels are nailed into place using annular-shanked nails, which have increased holding power and will, in most cases, not "pop" out after a few years. Nails are spaced approximately 8 inches apart. Nails are spaced 4 inches apart around the perimeter of each panel.

After the ceiling has been sheetrocked, cover panel joints and nailheads with Spackle and tape. You can then paint the ceiling or apply some other finish covering.

Because of its low cost and the ease with which it can be installed, Sheetrock is a valuable material, not only for the contractor and builder but for the home remodeler as well. If you have decided to finish off your basement or want to cure a problem ceiling in some other room in your home and your budget is a little lean, Sheetrock is the answer.

Since a ceiling is purely a cosmetic structure, it is common practice in new construction to use 1/4-inch Sheetrock on the ceiling joists. However, the thinner the Sheetrock panel, the more apparent will be the variations in the overall ceiling. When covering an existing ceiling in which the joists may not be exactly on the same plane (a very common occurrence), it will be necessary to user thicker sheets of Sheetrock. Panels 3/8 inch thick should cover most problems, but in extreme cases in which the joists are really out of plane, you should use 1/2-inch-thick Sheetrock panels.

PLANNING GYPSUM CEILINGS

As with any home remodeling project, the first place to begin is on a piece of paper. Thorough planning will make the job go quicker and help to eliminate unexpected problems.

Begin by making a scale drawing of the ceiling you are planning to cover with Sheetrock. Indicate the direction of the ceiling joists. Stretch a string tightly across the joists the full width of the room. The string will indicate the alignment of the joists, that is, whether or not they're on the same plane. If they are, the Sheetrock can be attached directly to them. But if the joists are not all on the same level, you may have to attach furring strips to some of them before attaching the Sheetrock. Make note of any required furring strips—on your drawing.

After you have a scale drawing on paper, with the joist direction indicated, you must decide how you want the panels to run—*across* the joists or *along* them. To make as little extra work for yourself as possible, you should plan the direction of the panels so there will be as few joints as possible. For example, in Fig. 7-1 a room 12 × 16 feet will require six 4-× 8-foot Sheetrock panels to cover the ceiling. In this sketch, two different panel placement plans are indicated: *With* the joists (A) and *across* the joists (B). With either plan six panels are needed to cover the ceiling, but plan A calls for a bit more work. I would choose plan B as the best way to attach the panels to the ceiling. Past experience has proven that joints tend to be stronger when the panels are attached *across* the joists rather than *with* them. In the long run this means that the joints between the boards have less chance of breaking or cracking.

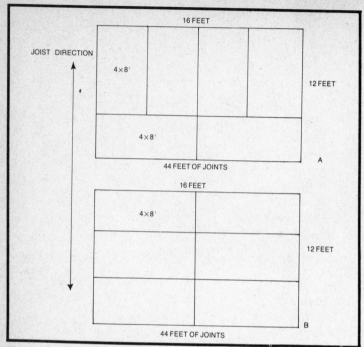

Fig. 7-1. Two panel patterns for a 12- by 16-foot ceiling.

TOOLS AND MATERIALS

In addition to the required number of Sheetrock panels, you will also need other materials and a few simple tools. Chances are, you already have all the tools you require, for they are necessary for most general home repairs and maintenance work.

Joint compound—ready mixed or powdered
Reinforcing tape
Open-grit sandpaper
*Annular-*or *ring-shanked wallboard nails*
4-foot steel ruler or *straightedge*
Utility knife with extra blades
Metal tape measure
Marking pencil
Stepladder
Surform tool
Hammer
Keyhole saw
4- or *6-inch-wide putty knife*
Furring strips (if needed)

SHEETROCKING THE CEILING

Sheetrock panels are packaged in pairs, the yellowish-white finished surfaces against one another and the gray backs exposed. To separate the sheets, tear the band of paper from each end. Care should be exercised when handling the Sheetrock panels because they damage easily. Corners of the panels will break if you drop them.

The floor of the room in which you will be working should be cleared of all furniture and swept before the panels are brought in. A cleared room is much easier to work in because the panels are bulky and you will be working overhead.

It doesn't matter if you are covering an entire room with Sheetrock or just the ceiling. The ceiling should be covered first. Get at least one other person to help you attach the Sheetrock panels to the ceiling. If you're working alone, you'll have to make a couple of T-braces. To make one, nail a 2-foot-long 1 × 4 to a 2 × 4 upright that is 1/2 inch longer than the ceiling height. Wedge the T-braces between floor and panel to support the panel while you're nailing it to the ceiling joists (Fig. 7-2).

Place each panel into position with the finish side out. Hold them tightly against the joists and nail them into place. Always nail from the center of the panel towards the edges, spacing the nails a maximum of 8 inches apart. Nail the perimeter of the panel last. Drive the nails through the panels (into the joists above) hard enough to leave dimples at each nailhead (Fig. 7-3). These dimple marks can be filled later with joint compound. Do not overdrive or countersink nails. This will break the face paper or fracture the core of the panel.

Most Sheetrocking jobs require that some of the panels be cut. Make all your cuts through the face of the panel, the finished side. Begin by measuring carefully; mark the panel with a pencil and straightedge. Then doublecheck your measurements to insure you are proceeding correctly. You can then cut the panel with your utility

Fig. 7-2. Using T-braces to wedge panels into place.

Fig. 7-3. Leave a dimple around each nailhead.

knife (Fig. 7-4). Hold the knife perpendicular to the panel and score the face surface paper along your mark. For long cuts, it might be helpful to use a straightedge or a straight 1 × 4 as a cutting guide. After the face paper has been scored about half way through (this may take a few passes with the knife), pick up the panel and fold backward. This will break the core along your cut. Fold back the partially separated portion of the board and use the knife to cut the back paper. The edges of the freshly cut panel should then be smoothed with a Surform tool. It is important that all edges of cut panels be kept as square as possible. If you don't have a Surform tool, you can smooth the panel edges with the edge of the utility knife blade.

Chances are, you will have to make a hole for an electrical outlet, heating duct, or some other ceiling fixture. Measure the exact location of the fixture and transfer the measurements to the face of the panel. Next, with a nail or awl, punch holes through the panel at the four corners of the fixture outline. Then with the knife, score the panel between the four holes. Turn the panel over and

Fig. 7-4. Slice the face paper of the panel with a utility knife.

score the back of the panel between the same four nail holes. When both sides of the panel have been scored around the hole, knock out the hole with a hammer.

You can also make a hole in Sheetrock with a keyhole saw. Just mark the exact location of the hole on the face of the panel, punch holes with a nail at the four corners, and then, with the keyhole saw, cut the hole.

As you place the Sheetrock panels into position, the edges should be against one another. If you must cut a panel for fit, remember that an exact fit is not necessary. Gaps up to 1 inch can be filled or covered with Spackle and tape after the panels have been attached.

Every edge of a Sheetrock panel should fall on the center of a joist. Standard spacing for ceiling joists is 16 or 24 inches, so the panels should end on a joist almost automatically.

To insure that the panel edges will rest on a joist, you should measure the distance from the previous panel to where the next panel will end to be sure that you will be in the center of a joist. In some cases you may have to either cut a panel or nail a 2 × 4 to the existing joists. Remember that *all* edges of a panel must be nailed to a joist.

TAPING AND SPACKLING

After you attach the Sheetrock panels to the ceiling joists, you will have a ceiling that is covered with nailheads, dimples, joints, spaces between panels, and possibly broken corners and gouges. All these blemishes must be filled with joint compound (also called Spackle). Some of the spaces and all the joints between the panels must be reinforced with perforated tape as well as joint compound.

Joint compound is available in either powder or premixed form. Personally, I prefer the premixed type because it is much easier to work with and requires no mixing. The powdered joint compound is less expensive, but the premixed joint compound is uniformly mixed to the right consistency. Simply open the can and use it.

Joints between the panels require the most work, so begin your spackling job with them. Plan on about 3 days for the job to be completed because each layer of Spackle must dry thoroughly before the next coat is applied.

Using a 4- or 5-inch-wide putty knife, spread the Spackle on a panel joint. While this first coat is still wet, press the perforated tape over the joint, smoothing the tape firmly into the wet joint compound with the putty knife until the compound underneath is forced through

Fig. 7-5. Press the tape into the joint compound.

the holes in the tape (Fig. 7-5). Apply enough pressure to make the tape lie flat on the surface of the ceiling, but make sure there is enough compound under the tape to insure a good bond. The joint compound acts as an adhesive for the tape. Cover the tape with an additional coat of compound and feather the edges of the tape with the putty knife. After this first coat has thoroughly dried (at least 24 hours), sand lightly to remove any sharp ridges or edges. Then apply the second coat, again feathering the edges of the joint for a flat smooth seam.

On the third day, sand lightly again and then apply the finish coat of joint compound, feathering the edges as you work. It will be helpful, on this last coat, if you use a putty knife with a very wide blade or, better yet, a 10-inch-wide joint finishing knife. The third coat is the finish coat, so when you are done, there should be no visible lines or seams. If necessary, you can sand lightly after the finish coat has dried, but sand carefully.

Nailheads, accompanying dimples, gouges, and any other recesses must also be filled with joint compound. For nailheads, first draw the bare putty knife over the nailheads. If you hear a metallic ring, drive the nailhead below the surface with a hammer. Working on one nailhead at a time, fill the dimples with compound, flush with the surface. Apply the joint compound with a sweep of the knife in one direction. Wipe off the excess compound with a sweep of the knife in the opposite direction, pressing out the excess until it is flush with the panel. After the first coat of joint compound has dried, sand lightly and apply a second and final coat of compound in the same manner. If necessary, nailhead coverings can be lightly sanded after the finish coat has dried.

Gouges and dents are handled in the same manner as nailheads: first coat, let dry, sand; final coat, let dry and then sand lightly, if necessary.

After you have completed the entire Spackle job and it is dry, look over the work. Apply an additional coat of joint compound to any areas that are not perfectly flat.

106

Never apply Spackle over partially dried areas. This will result in uneven drying that will surely crack at some later time. Joint compound should not be applied if the room temperature is below 50°F. Ideally, the room temperature should be around 65° to 70° F. Protect premixed joint compound from extreme heat and cold. The unused portion of joint compound will last for years if stored in the original container and kept tightly sealed. If, after opening the container of joint compound, you notice mold or mildew, remove this before using. If you notice that some of the liquid has separated from the joint compound, mix the batch thoroughly before using.

Spackling and taping is not necessary if you plan to cover your ceiling with paneling or other rigid ceiling coverings. Sanding of hardened joint compound is an extremely dusty process. Protect your home by keeping the room you are working in closed off to the rest of the house. Vacuum after sanding to prevent Spackle dust from being tracked all over your home. Of course, you can eliminate a lot of sanding by removing as much of the excess Spackle as possible while still wet. If you plan to paint your new ceiling, it is advisable to first give it a coat of primer. When this dries you can paint the ceiling usually with one coat.

Chapter 8
Textured Ceilings

Besides adding character, textured ceilings can be solutions to many ceiling problems. If your present ceilings sag, have falling plaster, or seem to be eye sores, you should consider installing textured ceilings as a way to give a room a whole new look (Fig. 8-1).

TYPES OF TEXTURED CEILINGS

A textured ceiling can be produced with sand paint, joint compound, painter's plaster, or textured ceiling tiles. Sand paint is the quickest and easiest to apply. Sand paint is, as the name implies, a mixture of latex, alkalyd or oil base paint, and fine-grain sand. It is applied to a ceiling in very much the same way you would apply conventional ceiling paint, with a roller or brush. The texture of sand paint is almost flat.

Another type of applied texture is possible using either joint compound or painter's plaster. Either one of these will enable you to give your ceiling a heavy texture. Probably the best example of heavy texture is stucco. Stucco ceilings (and walls) are rough textured and usually have a well defined pattern. It is also possible, using joint compound or painter's plaster, to create a texture that protrudes or "hangs" up to 1 inch from the ceiling. Such texture can be as bold, distinctive, and unique as you want it to be.

Painter's plaster is sold in powder form and must be mixed with water before application. Setup time is about 10 or 20 minutes, so you must work quickly, with small batches. Application is simple with a hand trowel and mortar board. Proper surface preparation is

Fig. 8-1. A textured ceiling.

important. Painter's plaster is buttered onto the ceiling with the trowel, and a texture pattern is added as the work progresses, before the plaster sets up.

Joint compound was originally developed for use on walls that have been covered with gypsum board. But joint compound also makes a fantastic texture medium. And because it takes several hours to dry and harden, it is extremely workable on ceilings. The long setup time and the fact that the joint compound is premixed are advantages that you will appreciate only after you have worked with painter's plaster.

Fig. 8-2. Another type of textured ceiling.

A third type of textured ceiling is possible using textured ceiling tiles. The textured ceiling tiles discussed in this chapter should not be confused with suspended ceiling tiles, which are covered in the next chapter. The ceiling tiles described here are attached directly to an existing ceiling (if the existing ceiling is sound) or to furring strips attached to the ceiling joists. Ceiling tiles are commonly 12 by 12 inches and have a tongue on two sides and a groove or slot on the other two sides. Tiles interlock with each other and are held to the ceiling with adhesive, staples, or nails. There are many different patterns and types of textured tiles available; you should pay a visit to your local home improvement center and look over the selection (Fig. 8-2).

Ceiling tile is highly porous. The perforations in the tile pattern are actually miniature sound traps. Noise enters these holes and is absorbed. This means that less sound is reflected than with conventional flat, plaster, or gypsum ceilings, resulting in a quieter room. Ceiling tiles can absorb as much as 50% of the noise that strikes them. Consider sound absorbing ceiling tiles for rooms such as the study, den, or playroom.

APPLIED TEXTURE

Surface preparation for sand paint, joint compound, or painter's plaster is basically the same. The surface of the ceiling must be clean, reasonably flat, and in sound condition. Loose paint should be removed and the surface should be sanded. Exposed nailheads, unprimed metal lath, and other base metal should be primed with a suitable metal primer before painting with sand paint. If the metal surfaces are not primed, they will "bleed" through the finished job. Ceiling water marks or stains should be sanded and primed before painting begins. If you are in doubt about whether or not the surface will show through the finished job, you should prime the area in question.

Working with sand paint is similar to working with any other interior paint, except that the paint is a bit thicker. When you are working with sand paint, or any paint for that matter, the finished job can only be as good as the surface preparation. Sand paint will cover hairline cracks and mask small nail holes. All other holes, cracks, or problem areas should be, as indicated above, patched with joint compound.

The tools and materials you will need to cover a ceiling with sand paint are:

Drop cloths
Roller handle, sleeve (designed for use with sand paint) *extension handle, and pan*
Two paint brushes —one 3-inch and one 4- or 5-inch
Stepladder
Sandpaper
Sand paint and tint (if you want a color other than off white)
Damp rag

As with any painting job, it is best to clear as much of the furniture, rugs, paintings, lamps, and other movable objects out of the room before surface preparation begins. After the room has been cleared, lay down drop cloths or old sheets to protect the floor. If you don't have any drop cloths or old sheets, you can lay newspapers down. But you should tape the pages together to prevent spreading. It is also a good idea to tape the paper to the wall where the baseboard meets. This will help to prevent the newspaper from moving and exposing the floor to paint drops.

I like to begin any ceiling painting job with a paint brush. I paint around the entire perimeter of the room at the wall-ceiling junction. These areas are the hardest to cover; such work requires a steady hand. After this area has been painted with a brush, the rest of the ceiling can be covered quickly with a roller.

Latex sand paint (the most common) is almost like any other latex base paint. The basic difference is that sand paint is thicker because of the addition of fine-grained sand. One gallon of sand paint will cover about one-half the area that 1 gallon of conventional latex paint will cover (approximately 250–300 square feet). When sand paint is applied to a ceiling, the paint will penetrate into the surface and the sand will remain on the surface. The sand is held on the surface by the latex paint, which acts like a glue. What you end up with is a surface that has been painted but is no longer flat, but textured. The resulting texture will depend on how much sand paint is put on the surface and what is done to the surface after the paint is applied. For example, you can paint the ceiling with a large paint brush; when the paint dries brush marks will be very apparent. Or you can paint the ceiling with a short-napped roller; the resultant texture will be uniform, almost flat but with grains of sand on the surface.

To paint the ceiling with a roller, I first fill the bottom of the paint tray with sand paint. Next, I slip a roller cover (designed for use with sand paint) on the roller. I screw on a roller handle, which can be a

---

CAPTIONS FOR FOLLOWING 4-PAGE COLOR SECTION

Plate 1. Here, the floor covering makes all the difference in the world. It's seamless, glossy, and perfectly matched to the earth colors in the room. (Courtesy Congoleum)

Plate 2. The floor coverings here are rich and luxuriously textured, the deep mauve carpet contrasting with the pale vinyl tiles of the hallway. (Courtesy NuTone)

Plate 3. The light-toned monochromatic ceilings help to accentuate the relatively bold statements of the patterned wall coverings. Combinations power vent and light fixtures are functional addition to do-it-yourself bathroom remodeling. (Courtesy NuTone)

Plate 4. These schemes are alive with complementary shades and textures, and the most notable complementaries are the light-colored plank ceilings and the intricately patterned tile flooring. (Courtesy Armstrong)

broom handle that has a threaded tip. Such an extension handle for the roller is necessary for painting ceilings and will make any roller painting job easier. The roller is rolled into the paint in the bottom of the paint tray until the roller is evenly coated with sand paint. I begin rolling paint onto the ceiling using short strokes. Because sand paint is so much thicker than conventional latex paint, you will not be able, nor should you try, to cover very much area with a roller full of paint. Roll the sand paint on to cover small areas approximately 2 by 3 feet. By working in a small area, you can put enough sand paint on the ceiling to cover *and* add texture.

About the only tools that can be used effectively to add texture to a freshly sand painted ceiling are paint brushes, textured rollers, or wide wallpaper brushes.

The use of a paint brush will give you a sweeping texture as wide as the paint brush. If you are using a 4-inch paint brush, for example, you will be able to add 4-inch texture strokes to the ceiling. If you are painting a large ceiling, it is sometimes a good idea to paint the entire ceiling with a wide paint brush and add texture as you apply the paint. This method will save a lot of time because you are adding texture as you go along, but painting overhead with a paint brush is not easy work.

To get the most uniform type of texture on a ceiling, it is best to use a textured roller. Textured rollers enable you to add texture as you apply the paint. Basically there are two types of textured roller sleeves: short- and long-napped. A short-napped roller will give a texture that is relatively flat, while the texture from a long-napped roller will be heavier, more prominent.

A wallpaper brush can be used in conjunction with a textured roller to give a texture similar to that which you can achieve with a wide paint brush. The basic difference is that with a wallpaper brush, the texture sweeps are larger, say 12 to 18 inches.

The textures created with sand paint can be in the form of long sweeping lines, swirls, arcs, curves, and just about any other design you can come up with using a brush. Sand painting is the quickest way to add texture to your ceiling; it produces texture that is relatively subtle.

If you want heavy texture, or if your ceiling has a lot of cracks or holes, then your best bet is to cover the ceiling with joint compound. Joint compound comes premixed in 5-gallon cans. Cost is usually around $10, but you can get a lot of mileage from one can.

Surface preparation before using joint compound is similar to surface preparation for sand painting. Large cracks, holes, and irregularities in the ceiling should be patched, keeping in mind that two light fillings are far superior to a single heavy one. Allow sufficient time for the first fill to dry before adding the second. Small cracks and holes need not be repaired before plastering the entire ceiling; they can be filled as you apply the texture coat. All stains, water marks, bare metal, bare wood, and darkly painted areas should be primed, for it is possible that these areas will bleed through the texture. Another reason for priming these areas is that the plaster may not adhere well on these surfaces. If in doubt, prime.

To texture a ceiling with joint compound, you'll need drop cloths, a stepladder, a scrap piece of plywood (2-feet square) which will be used as a pallet, a large wall scraper, a trowel or putty knife, and some type of texture tool.

Since joint compound takes around an hour to harden, you have time to form it into the type of texture you want. You can create texture with damp sponges, rakes, long-napped rollers with ropes wrapped around the sleeves, wet burlap, shaped objects, and almost anything else that can be pressed into the wet joint compound to form an impression. It makes good sense to try several different tools or objects on a scrap piece of plywood; this way you can perfect the type of texture you want. Once you have developed the type of heavy texture you want, you can add that texture to your ceiling.

After all surface preparations have been satisfactorily performed, you can begin applying the joint compound to the ceiling. Begin in a corner and work your way to the center of the room. I have found it easiest to work with about 2 pounds of joint compound on the plywood pallet. I apply the compound to the ceiling with a wide smooth trowel, buttering it on the ceiling. After I have covered as large an area as possible, without moving the ladder, I add the texture or leave the buttered-on effect. I continue to work in sections of the room until the entire ceiling has been covered with joint compound and textured. Stop often and look over the work to make sure that the texture is uniform. An average 9- by 12-foot ceiling can usually be textured with joint compound in less than 3 hours.

Painter's plaster is applied in much the same way as joint compound.

TEXTURED CEILING TILE

If your existing ceiling has noticeable recesses and cracks, or if you want some noise insulating value in your new ceiling, then ceiling tile is for you. Ceiling tile is relatively easy to install. An average size room (9 by 12 feet, for example) can be covered in less than a day. Begin by estimating your material needs.

First you must decide how you will attach the tile to your ceiling. There are two fastenings: staples and adhesive. The condition of your existing ceiling will determine how you attach the tile.

Furring strips (1- by 2-inch wooden strips) can be nailed directly to wood joists or through the existing ceiling into the joists to provide an evenly spaced framework to staple the tiles to (Fig. 8-3). You should use the furring strip method if (1) the existing ceiling is Sheetrock nailed to joists spaced more than 16 inches on-center, or (2) if the existing ceiling is in need of repair (i.e., chipped, peeling, holes, or cracks).

Determine the length and width of your ceiling and purchase the required number of tiles to do the job. As insurance against mistakes, you should purchase extra tiles. Since standard ceiling tiles are 12 by 12 inches, estimating the required number of tiles is fairly simple. If your room measures 9 by 12 feet, you will need 108 tiles to do the job ($9 \times 12 = 108$). If you are planning to attach the tile to furring strips, you will need ten 12-foot-long strips for this room.

The tools and materials you will need to install ceiling tiles are:

Hammer and nails —for attaching furring strips
Staple gun and staples
Stepladder
Saw or *sharp utility knife* —for cutting tile
Straightedge
Chalk line and ruler
Adhesive and brush —if using this method

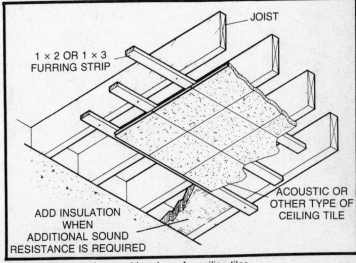

Fig. 8-3. Furring strips provide a base for ceiling tiles.

Fig. 8-4. Low spots can be brought up to true by driving shims between joists and furring strips.

Begin by clearing everything that is movable out of the room: furniture, lamps, area rugs, etc. Cover the floor with drop cloths. If lighting fixtures are attached to the ceiling, they should be removed and placed aside.

The furring strips should be attached perpendicular to the existing joists and spaced 12 inches on-center (Fig. 8-3). Place the first furring strip flush against the wall, at right angles to the ceiling joists. If joists are concealed by an existing ceiling, mark their location before work begins. They are usually spaced 16 inches on-center, perpendicular to the long wall of the room.

The second furring strip should be placed parallel to the first and spaced 12 inches on-center. Continue attaching the furring strips across the ceiling, at 12-inch intervals, until the entire ceiling has been covered.

After the strips are attached to the joists, insure they are level by checking them with a straightedge. If they aren't level, wedge shims between the strips and joists (Fig. 8-4). Scrap pieces of 1/4-inch plywood or tapered shingles make excellent shims.

Begin installing the ceiling tiles in a corner, working along one wall. In most cases the first row of tile has to be face nailed close to the edge of the wall. Later, these nailheads can be concealed by molding. The tongue edge of the tile is placed against the wall; the groove edge is stapled to the second furring strip. Staple twice on both grooves.

The second tile's tongue is inserted into the first tile's groove and then stapled. As you slide the tiles into position, make sure they join snugly; but do not force them. The last course, against the wall, will have to be face nailed, as the first course was. The nailheads can be concealed with molding.

To cut tiles, use a sharp utility knife to score the face deeply, then break the tile over a straightedge. Trim the back of the tile after breaking. If you prefer to use a saw, score the face of the tile and then saw through. The saw should have at least 12 teeth to an inch for a smooth-edged cut.

If your existing ceiling is in good condition, you can install the ceiling tiles with adhesive. You must first snap chalk lines across the ceiling to indicate tile layout. The location of the reference lines is determined by the size of the tile, usually 12 × 12 inches. Snap reference lines across the entire ceiling.

Place five daubs of ceiling tile adhesive on the back of each tile, one at each corner and one in the center of the tile. Each daub of adhesive should be about 1 1/2 inches across and at least the thickness of a quarter. Do not apply the adhesive close to the edge; it may ooze when the tile is pressed into position. A 1-inch paint brush makes an ideal adhesive applier.

The first, or border, tile is slipped into position in a corner and pressed up tightly against the ceiling. It is a good idea to put two staples in the flange of the tile to hold it in position while the adhesive sets. Apply adhesive to subsequent tiles and attach to the ceiling, using the chalk lines as a reference. Continue until the entire ceiling has been covered with tile. As you proceed, keep checking that the tiles are interlocked tightly and aligned with previous tiles. The job should be finished off with cover molding around the perimeter of the room (Fig. 8-5).

Under normal conditions textured ceiling tiles will remain new looking without any maintenance at all. As time goes on, however, tiles may become soiled or damaged, and you will want to restore the

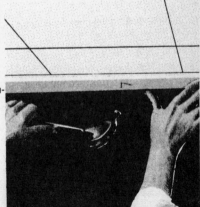

Fig. 8-5. Cover molding is the finishing touch.

ceiling. Ceiling tiles, like all building materials, vary in composition and finish, so you should bear this in mind before attempting to clean or paint.

Loose dirt and dust can usually be removed with a soft brush, working carefully so you won't damage the finish on the tile. A vacuum cleaner with a soft brush attachment might be used. This type of maintenance will clean most surface dirt and dust.

Small spots or streaks can usually be removed with an art gum eraser. You can usually pick one up at a stationery store. Larger smudges can usually be removed with wallpaper cleaner available at hardware stores, wallpaper stores, and some supermarkets. These cleaners, either putty or paste type, should be used carefully. For nicks and scratches you can sometimes do a satisfactory repair job with colored chalk.

Many types of textured ceiling tiles can be washed providing that reasonable care is exercised. There are, however, a few simple rules that must be followed for best results:

1. Use a mild soap, such as white soap flakes or white facial soap. Suds up the soap with warm water. Some mild detergents can also be used but should be tested first on an inconspicuous spot.
2. Never soak ceiling tiles with water. Use a *damp* cloth or sponge. Wipe the face of the tile in long sweeping, gentle strokes. Too much water may warp the tile.
3. Rinse the tiles by wiping with a damp cloth or sponge.
4. If the tiles have been installed with adhesive, it is desirable to postpone cleaning or painting for at least 90 days. This waiting period gives the adhesive time to properly set. This also reduces the danger of warping as a result of excessive wetting or of moving the tile through excessive pressure.

By following these simple guidelines, your textured tile ceiling should give you years of good service.

Chapter 9
Suspended Ceilings

A suspended ceiling consists of ceiling panels supported in place by a metal framework, or lattice. This type of ceiling was first widely used in businesses but is now used often in houses. There are many good reasons for the widespread acceptance. Suspended ceilings are easy to install; a 12- by 12-foot room can be remodeled with a suspended ceiling in just a few hours, using only a few common tools. Suspended ceilings cover up problems such as cracked plaster and sagging ceilings. Suspended ceilings provide added insulating value, and they absorb up to 75% of the noise from either side of the panel. These properties help to prevent heat loss and make the room more comfortable. Suspended ceilings can be easily set into place and removed. This enables homeowners to remove the panels for cleaning. And the ease with which the panels can be cleaned eliminate the need for painting. The panels are available in a variety of textures and styles. There is a pattern for every room in your home, from simple flat panels to embossed, highly decorative panels.

THE FACTS ABOUT SUSPENDED CEILINGS

The panels themselves are commonly available in two sizes: 2 by 2 feet and 2 by 4 feet. They are made from either wood fiber or fiberglass and are faced with either vinyl, for easy cleaning, or white paint. Panels are easily cut with a sharp knife or a fine-toothed saw. Even the 2- by 4-foot panels are lightweight and can easily be set into place by one person.

All lattice systems are basically the same. They usually consist of wall-angle aluminum bars and T-shaped rails. The wall-angle bars

Fig. 9-1. Installing wall-angle bars.

are L shaped and are attached to the walls around the entier perime-ter of the room (Fig. 9-1). The wall-angle bars are the guides for the rest of the ceiling, so special care must be exercised during their installation to insure that these sections are level and on the same plane.

The T-shaped aluminum rails form the lattice. There are two kinds: main tees and cross tees. Main tees span the room and hook onto the wall-angle bars (Fig. 9-2). The main tees are held in position by suspension wires attached to the existing ceiling joists. The main tees support the cross tees and the ceiling panels, so the main tees must be hung at right angles to the joists above. Main tees are notched at intervals so the cross tees can be interlocked (Fig. 9-3).

Cross tees are available in 2- and 4-foot lengths and are installed between the main tees. The panels are fitted into the lattice work (Fig. 9-4).

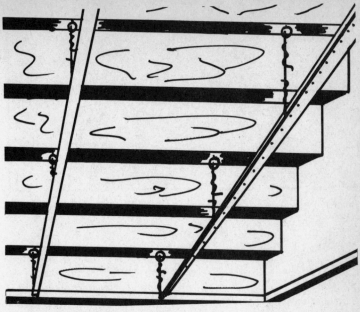

Fig. 9-2. Main tees span the room.

PLANNING YOUR SUSPENDED CEILING

Planning your ceiling is probably the single most important step of installing a suspended ceiling in your home. Careful planning will give you an indication of the materials you will require for the job, make the actual installation go quicker, and assure a finished job with professional looking results.

First measure the dimensions of your room carefully and transfer these distances to a piece of graph paper. Make a scale drawing of the room. Indicate all extensions, alcoves, closets, lighting fixtures, etc. Note the direction of the ceiling joists.

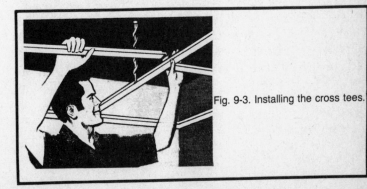

Fig. 9-3. Installing the cross tees.

Fig. 9-4. Angle the ceiling panels through the opening and drop them into position.

Determine how far you want to lower your ceiling. You may install a ceiling that is 2 inches below your present ceiling—or several feet. A 2-inch minimum space is required, however, between the existing ceiling and the new installation. The new ceiling must be below any heating ducts, pipes, or electrical connections.

Calculate the number of panels you'll need. Here's a sample calculation. Let's assume that a room measures 10 by 12 feet. If the panels (2 by 4 feet) will be set into place with the 4-foot sides parallel to the longest wall, then we would divide the length of the room (12 feet) by 4 (Fig. 9-5). We would then have three rows of panels. Next, we would divide the width of the room (10 feet) by 2 feet (the width of each panel). This would show that there would be five panels in each row. Multiply the number of rows (3) by the number of panels in each row (5) to arrive at the total number of ceiling panels needed (3 × 5 = 15 panels).

On the graph paper, indicate where the main tees will be located. Remember that these must always be at right angles to the joists and are always 4 feet apart. Next, determine where the cross tees will be located. They should be 2 feet apart, at right angles to the main tees, parallel to the joists.

Based on the measurements you mark down on the graph paper, you can determine your material needs. For the 10- by 12-foot room (Fig. 9-5), we would need the following materials:

Wall-angle bars	*44 feet*
Main tees	*20 feet*
Cross tees	*48 feet*
Screw eyes and wire	*15 feet*

In addition to these materials, you will need a few simple hand tools:

Hammer
Measuring tape
Chalk line
Level
Ladder
Pliers
Utility knife
Hacksaw

Though it may be true that a suspended ceiling can be installed in just a few hours, you should be prepared to invest as much time as needed to obtain professional looking results. If you plan to paint the walls of the room, you should do this *before* beginning the ceiling

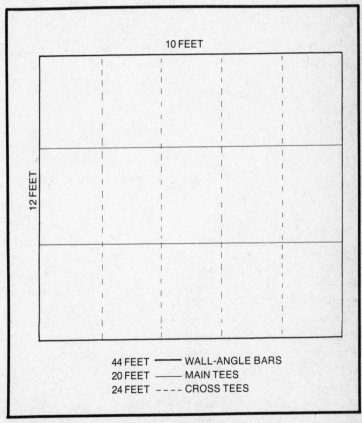

Fig. 9-5. Typical layout for a suspended ceiling.

project. Start by removing everything from the room: chairs, tables, lamp fixtures, whatever can be moved. When the room is as bare as possible, you can begin the installation of the new suspended ceiling.

INSTALLING A SUSPENDED CEILING

The first step is to establish a ceiling height, keeping in mind that additional lowering may be necessary for heating ducts and other protrusions from the existing ceiling. When the height has been determined, mark a level line on all the walls using a chalk line. Next, align the bottom flange of the wall-angle aluminum bars with the chalk line and attach them to the wall with appropriate fasteners (Fig. 9-1). If you are nailing, nail through the wall-angle bars and into the wall studs. Common stud spacing is 16 or 24 inches on-center. Use screw anchors or concrete nails for masonry walls, and suitable expansion or toggle bolts for plaster walls.

After the wall-angle aluminum bars have been attached around the entire perimeter of the room, install the main tees. Snap a chalk line across the joists where the first main tee is to positioned. Repeat this procedure, in accordance with your layout plan, for the remaining tees. From the first joist from the wall, suspend a 12-gauge galvanized hanger wire at each chalk line, using a tenpenny nail or screw eye (Fig. 9-2). Suspend hanger wires from other joists (a maximum of 48 inches apart, at the chalk marks).

After you have attached the required number of hanger wires, you must insure that they're on the same plane, at the correct level. The best way to accomplish this is by using a guide string. Stretch a string between parallel wall-angle bars, perpendicular to the ceiling joists, at the exact location of the main tee. The string must be on the same plane as the wall-angle bars. Next, bend each wire with a pair of pliers so it will just meet the string.

When all the suspension wires have been bent to the level of the string, you can begin installing the main tees. Cut the main tees to the appropriate length. Thread the bent wires through the holes in the main tees and secure by wrapping excess wire around the vertical wire. Repeat for each main tee until all have been securely fastened to the ceiling joists.

Now you can install the cross tees. These will be 2-foot rails that interlock with the main tees at 4-foot intervals. Interlocking spacer holes are usually located at 6-inch intervals on the main tees (Fig. 9-3).

Cross tees that have one end resting on wall-angle bars are called border tees. The installation is simple. First measure the distance from the main tee to the wall, allowing 1/8 inch for wall-angle bar thickness. Next, cut the cross tee at the right length and install by inserting the cross tee connector into the main tee slot. Rest the cut end of the cross tee on the wall-angle bar. After all the cross tees and border tees have been cut (where necessary) and set into place, you can install the ceiling panels.

Begin installing the ceiling panels by cutting the border panels and laying them in place. Panels should be cut face up on a flat surface. For best results, take careful measurements and use a metal ruler (or scrap piece of tee) and a sharp razor knife.

After all the border panels have been cut and laid in place, install the remainder of the panels (Fig. 9-4). Exercise care when handling ceiling panels to avoid marring their surface. Hold the *edges* of the panels, keeping the fingers off the finished side as much as possible. Though most panels are washable, don't make unnecessary work for yourself.

Occasionally you will have to custom fit panels around obstructions like columns, ventilation and heating ducts, and lighting fixtures.

Begin by accurately measuring the exact location of the obstruction in relation to the panel. Transfer an outline of the obstruction to the face of the panel. Carefully cut along the outline with a fine-tooth keyhole saw or sharp utility knife. The cutout should be slightly smaller than the obstruction—to insure a tight fit. It may be necessary to cut the panel into two parts to install it around the obstruction. The pieces can then be inserted into place one at a time.

LIGHTING AND SUSPENDED CEILINGS

Lighting for most suspended ceilings consists of an opaque panel (instead of a ceiling panel) with a light fixture behind it. Fluorescent lighting fixtures are the only type recommended by all suspended ceiling manufactuers because of the low heat.

Most suspended ceiling manufacturers offer fluorescent lighting fixtures in standard ceiling panel sizes. The fixtures themselves usually attach to the ceiling joists and provide lighting for an entire room. Usually a 5-inch head space must be available for proper installation. The luminous opaque panels are usually available in textures that will match the surrounding ceiling panels. Armstrong, for example, offers over 10 different textures of luminous panels. These textured styrene panels are made from a nonyellowing plastic.

The lighting fixtures should be installed after the basic lattice has been constructed. Electrical connections, however, should not be attempted unless you are familiar with electrical circuitry. A qualified electrician should be called in for the final hookup. After all electrical connections have been completed, you can drop the plastic panel into place. Plastic luminous panels and lighting fixtures can be used throughout the suspended ceiling for a completely unique and functional lighting system. When you shop for a suspended ceiling, ask the salesman about recessed lighting.

CARING FOR YOUR SUSPENDED CEILING

The lattice for a suspended ceiling is designed to hold up the ceiling panels. You should never hang any heavy objects from the system. Lightweight party or holiday decorations, however, can be hung easily from the framework. But always hang these decorations from the tees, not from the ceiling panels.

Once a suspended ceiling has been properly installed, it should give years of service with no maintenance at all. You will have eliminated the ceiling painting problem because most ceiling panels are vinyl faced and can be wiped clean with a damp cloth. Periodic cleaning is the only maintenance required. If a panel is heavily soiled, try using a mild liquid cleaner, but never any type of abrasive cleanser. If a panel should become stained or heavily soiled beyond cleaning, replace it.

Chapter 10
Wood Ceilings

Wood ceilings are coming back into vogue—for good reasons. The natural beauty of a wood ceiling conveys a feeling of warmth. Besides that, wood insulates well. If a wood ceiling is installed correctly and finished with some type of protective coating, such as varnish or polyurethane, little or no maintenance will be required. Wood ceilings can help hide flawed surfaces, and the wood itself is hard to damage.

Covering an interior ceiling with wood can be expensive. Milled lumber (boards that have been planed on four sides) is the most costly. But there are other alternatives for the homeowner in search of wood for his interior ceilings. These include rough-cut lumber, wood-grained ceiling tiles, imitation beams (made from Styrofoam), plywood paneling, and recycled lumber.

MILLED-LUMBER CEILINGS

The following is the procedure for installing a typical milled-lumber ceiling (in this case, redwood lumber, 6 and 8 inches wide, tongue-and-groove).

Determine the dimensions of the room and draw a sketch of the ceiling. On the sketch indicate the direction of the joists, joist spacing, alcoves, hallways, or anything else that influences the shape of the ceiling. Buy enough redwood lumber to cover the ceiling (and an additional 10% to cover mistakes). You will also need molding to finish the job. Store the lumber in the house so the lumber can acclimate itself to the relative humidity of the house.

Surface preparation is usually limited to removing existing moldings at the junction of the walls and ceiling. If there is falling plaster, you should remove as much as possible. Holes, peeling paint, stains, etc. will be covered with the lumber.

As with other ceiling remodeling projects, everything that can be moved out of the room should be. Next, the location and direction of the joists should be clearly marked. Strike chalk lines across the entire ceiling to indicate the position of joists.

If you are covering the ceiling in an unfinished attic, you should install insulation between the rafters *before* covering the ceiling with milled lumber. You might also consider installing a vapor barrier or foil for added insulation.

Either nails or adhesive can be used to attach milled lumber to ceilings. Personally, I think that a combination of the two fastenings is best. I attach the boards at right angles to the joists and nail them at each joist location. But before I raise each piece of lumber into position, I apply a bead of mastic adhesive with a caulking gun to the back of the board. Next, I slide each board's tongue into the previous board's groove and press it into place against the ceiling. I then drive one nail through the groove of the board at each joist location.

Working overhead like this can be made less of a chore if someone helps you. A helper can apply adhesive to the back of a board and hand it to you. Then you both can raise the board into position and make sure it is tightly joined to the adjacent board. Your helper can hold the board in place while you nail it to the joists.

An additional aid is a type of scaffold made from a 12-inch-wide plank (2 × 12) around 10 to 12 feet long and resting on top of several steel milk crates.

Nails should be long enough to pass through the grooves of the boards, through any existing ceiling covering (plaster or Sheetrock), and into the joists. You should use a nailset to drive the head of the nail flush with the bottom of the groove. Since most milled lumber is straight, you should not have any problem aligning the joints between the boards.

Wood ceilings are most commonly finished off with decorative molding. As with baseboards, ceiling moldings should also be cope jointed. This insures a tight joint and a good fit—even when humidity is high. Finish nails should be driven into the upper wall plates and also into the ceiling joists for large moldings. Then the nailheads should be countersunk or set with a nailset. If desired, the resulting nailhole can be filled with a matching filler made from white glue and sawdust from the lumber being used.

ALTERNATIVE WOOD CEILINGS

There are, of course, less costly alternatives to milled lumber. These include square-edged lumber, recycled materials, plywood, wall paneling, and wood textured ceiling tiles. If your budget is really limited, you might consider building wooden or imitation beams for your ceiling. There is even an imitation (Styrofoam) type of beam that looks very much like the real thing.

Square-edged boards are probably the most common type of building material in existence. For ceilings the boards must be face nailed, but if finishing nails are used and the heads are countersunk, the nails will be hard to see.

You are not limited to straight runs with wood ceilings; you can run boards *diagonally* across the ceiling. Other possibilities include the herringbone style or a collage effect. The possibilities are limited only by your imagination.

If you live around a saw mill, you may be able to buy rough-cut lumber at a bargain price. Usually, the mill price for rough-cut lumber is around half the cost of milled or square-edged lumber. Rough-cut lumber is lumber that has been cut into common sizes (1 × 6 for example) but has not been surfaced or planed. These boards are usually squared off and are full measurements. For example, a 1 × 6 board actually measures 1 inch thick by 6 inches wide, not 3/4 by 5 3/4 inches.

Rough-cut lumber is rustic looking, but you may have a room in your house that would look good with a rustic ceiling. There is, however, one caution. Rough-cut lumber will be green when you first get it; that is, the moisture content will be high. If the boards are attached in this state, they will shrink in a short time. It's better to store the boards for a few months out of the weather so they can cure properly. It is advisable to stack the boards with spacers between them to permit air circulation. After about 3 months you can attach the boards to your ceiling and not have to worry about any major shrinkage.

Plywood wall paneling can also be attached to your ceiling. There are so many different paneling patterns, styles, and textures that you can surely find one that is right for your ceiling. The only problem with wall paneling is that it is usually sold in 4- by 8-foot sheets. Most rooms are considerably larger, and this means that you will have to do something with the joints between the panels. One possibility is to use beams to cover the seams.

If you don't care for planks or plywood, you can install wood-grained ceiling tiles. These tiles come packed in cartons containing

Fig. 10-1. A ceiling accented with prefinished wooden beams.

three different width tiles in lengths of 4 and 6 feet. The tiles, which come in two colors, an off-white and a dark wood grain, look very much like wooden planks. These ceiling tiles can be installed using either the staple or adhesive method.

If your decorating plans are limited by a tight budget, you can still achieve a custom ceiling by using recycled materials. There are several ways you can cover any ceiling in your home for practically nothing, providing you have some time and a strong desire to create a distinctive looking interior ceiling. Some possible recyclable materials include old barn siding, wall and ceiling paneling from an old house, crating...Just about anything you can get your hands on can give a new look to your ceiling.

Some companies are now manufacturing "old" barn siding, and it is a good imitation of the real thing. It's available in 8- or 10-foot lengths and widths ranging from 4 to 10 inches. This type of barn siding is much easier to work with. Simply buy and install. However, the cost is on the heavy side—around a dollar for an 8-foot-long 1 × 6!

Crating and pallets are made from rough-sawn softwood. This wood comes in many different sizes and is often discarded by factories and stores. Working with crating usually requires a lot of work because crates often take a beating in transit. A belt sander will be of great help in cleaning up the boards before you attach them to your ceiling.

If you want wood on your ceiling but don't have a lot of time or money to spend, consider installing wooden beams. There are three kinds: solid beams, constructed beams, and imitation beams.

Exposed beams, or timbers as they are sometimes called, are very popular in American homes (Fig. 10-1). It is entirely possible to install beams on your present ceiling, but the work may involve adding extra ceiling joists or some type of bracing system to carry the extra load.

Practically the only way to install real beams to an existing ceiling is to attach them to the joists. This will involve drilling holes in the beams at the joist locations and screwing the beams to the joists with heavy-duty screws. The screw holes can then be filled with pegs cut from 1-inch dowels.

One alternative to real beams are box beams, which are built onto the ceiling (Fig. 10-2). First a 2 × 4 is attached to the ceiling, perpendicular to the joists and across the entire room. Then 1 × 4 or 1 × 6 square-edged lumber is attached to the 2 × 4 to form a box like structure. The top edges of the 1 × 4 or 1 × 6 should be beveled slightly to make them easier to refinish when necessary (Fig. 10-3).

If you want to give the box beam a distressed (aged or roughed) look, you can shape the boards before they are attached to the

2 × 4. Use a small hand ax to chip off pieces of the board. Work carefully because an ax can take huge chunks off the board before you know what's happening. Another way to distress boards (or beams) is with a length of chain. Simply beat the board with the chain until you have the desired effect. You might find it easier to stain or finish the boards *before* you attach them to the ceiling.

Fig. 10-2. Typical ceiling box beams.

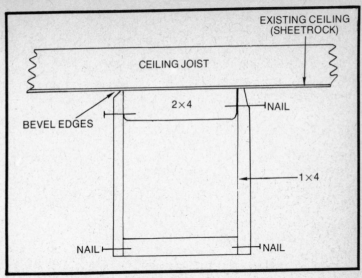

Fig. 10-3. Anatomy of a simple box beam.

Barclay Industries, Inc. manufactures wooden beams for installation on interior ceilings (Fig. 10-1). These beams are made from solid lumber and are hand distressed.

Before installing these beams you should insure that the ceiling structure is in good condition and will support the required load. Installation is simple. The beams are manufactured with a 3-inch hollow to accomodate a 1- × 3-inch or 2- × 3-inch furring strip. Therefore, the first step is to attach furring strips across the joists. If you want the beams to run parallel to your existing joists, the furring strips can be attached to the ceiling with toggle bolts, every 24 inches.

The next step is to press the beams firmly over the furring strips and secure them with eightpenny finishing nails, approximately 16 inches apart.

No maintenance is required with these beams; however, if any damage occurs during installation, you can use ordinary brown shoe polish to touch up the area.

Barclay also manufactures authentic urethane reproductions of rustic, hand-hewn beams. These beams measure 4 by 6 inches and are available in lengths of 12, 14, and 16 feet. Installation is the simplest of any type of beam. Cut the beams to size; then using a caulking gun, apply a 1/4-inch continuous bead of adhesive to the back of the beam. Next, press the beam into position on a clean, dry ceiling. The manufacturer claims that an entire room can be beamed in just a few hours.

Chapter 11
Lighting

Room lighting can not only be functional, but aesthetic. Lighting sets the mood of a room and can create certain decorative effects. To get the full advantage of a decorating scheme, it is important to place lights in areas of emphasis. Every surface in the home reflects some of the light it receives. Light can be absorbed and even wasted on some dark surfaces, or it can be reflected by lighter surfaces and used in indirect ways.

TYPES OF LIGHTING

Interior lighting comes in three forms: incandescent, fluorescent, and the aluminized reflector lamp.

Incandescent lighting is the most common form of artificial interior lighting. Incandescent light is the brilliant glow emitted by an intensely hot metal filament—usually tungsten—encased in glass with an inert gas, as in the common screw-in light bulb. Such lighting is dependable, easy to use, and relatively inexpensive. Incandescent light bulbs have a life of approximately 1000 hours. It has a multidirectional distribution of light; that is, the light comes out from the entire surface of the bulb shape. The most common household incandescent light bulbs range from 15 to 200 watts in power consumption.

Three-way incandescent light bulbs have two filaments. Each can be operated separately or in combination with the other. First, the low-wattage filament is switched on separately; when switched again, the low-wattage filament goes off and the high-wattage filament comes on. When switched on again, both low- and high-wattage filaments come on together to give three lighting effects. The three-way bulb is an excellent energy saver.

Fluorescent lamps have become well established as light sources in American homes. Since they were first introduced in 1938, fluorescent lights have found their way into over half the homes in the country.

Fluorescent lighting is efficient and economical. Light output is three times greater than that of conventional incandescent light bulbs. For example, one 4-foot fixture with two 40-watt fluorescent tubes is more efficient to use and produces more light than one 150-watt incandescent bulb, or two 75-watt incandescent bulbs.

Fluorescent lighting can be used effectively in every room of the home, and the lamps which are available are flattering to complexions and furnishings. To make every watt count, fluorescents can be used to replace incandescents over the workbench, in the bathroom, and in the kitchen.

Fluorescent tubes, unlike incandescent lamps, require special electrical equipment to operate properly. However, the savings from efficiency and longer life can pay back the cost of this extra equipment. A fluorescent fixture commonly consists of a metal channel that contains the wiring, the ballast for regulating the flow of current, and the lampholders or sockets. In past years, most fixtures for household use also required a starter, which is a small,

Fig. 11-1. Dimmer switches can be installed using just a screwdriver.

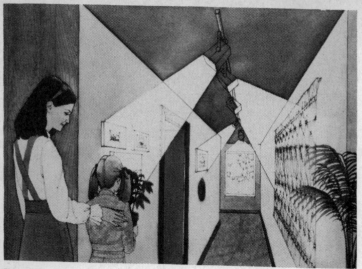

Fig. 11-2. A typical track lighting system.

cylindrical device that aids in starting the lamp when it is switched on. Now, however, most modern fixtures are equipped with a "trigger start" or "rapid start" circuit which results in very little, if any, delay in starting.

Dimmer switches (Fig. 11-1) are available for 30-watt and 40-watt fluorescent tubes and can help create different background lighting for different uses. One added advantage of dimming fluorescent lights is that they do not change color as much as incandescent bulbs when they are dimmed.

Aluminized reflector lamps are the third type of lighting used in modern homes. These lamps are used mainly for track lighting. They have built in reflecting surfaces which push the light out from the source. The bulb of each lamp is thick heat-resistant, or "hard," glass. It is a mold-pressed unit. The filaments of these lamps are rigidly mounted at the focal points of the precisely formed reflectors. Conventional incandescent lamps are less expensive than these, but they have shorter lives; about 750 hours compared to approximately 2000 hours for the more expensive aluminized reflector lamps.

You will encounter six beam designations for aluminized reflector lamps: very narrow spot, narrow spot, spot, flood, wide flood, and very wide flood.

Narrow spots are designed to throw intense, narrow light beams for medium to long-range spotlighting, or they can throw high-intensity spotlighting at closer range.

Flood lamps are recommended for shorter distances and general-area floodlighting with a medium to low intensity.

Wide floods are designed to spread broad, uniform beams over a wide area.

Very wide floods have a beam spread almost twice as wide, and there is no "hotspot" in the beam.

TRACK LIGHTING

Track lighting is not new. You have been seeing it in retail stores and shops for years (Fig. 11-2). What is new about track lighting is its use in the home to help create different atmospheres. Interior decorators long ago discovered the flexibility of track lighting and, to a large extent, have been responsible for its increased use in houses.

Track lighting is a method of lighting that takes up no floor or table space. It can light up an entire room or a selected area. There are no lamp cords to trip over, and the lights themselves are generally out of the reach of children.

Track lighting, as the name implies, consists of a grooved track with attached lamps (Fig. 11-3). The groove of the track is a circuit

Fig. 11-3. Two tracks with attached lamps.

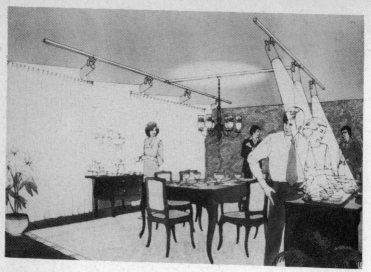

Fig. 11-4. A typical track pattern.

that provides current to the lamps. The track is fixed to the ceiling or wall with toggle bolts, screws, or spacer clips.

Tracks can be installed in just about any configuration. Various configurations are possible because of track connectors. Connectors do just what their name implies: They electrically connect various lengths of track.

Into a track you can insert any number of track lights. Track lights are movable on the track so you can change their position simply and quickly.

Track lights are also flexible. They rotate from side to side or pivot up and down so you can direct the beam of light in precisely the area you want it.

Today there are several manufacturers of track lighting systems, and the components of one system are not necessarily interchangeable with another. So examine closely every facet of the system you decide to use, both for quality and ease with which you can install and operate it.

Originally all track lighting was one circuit. It contained one "hot" wire; when the track was turned on, *all* the lights on that track came on. Gradually, as track lighting became more popular, multicircuit tracks were developed to provide greater versatility. Now it is possible to have up to three different circuits in one track (Fig. 11-5). A three-circuit track lighting system enables you to use three different groups of lights independently. The choice of a one-circuit or three-circuit track system depends entirely on what you want your track lighting to do. Before the development of three-circuit tracks, three different installations of one-circuit track were necessary to do the work of one three-circuit track system.

Tracks are available in 2-foot, 4-foot, and 8-foot lengths. The better tracks can be cut to any desired length with a hacksaw (Fig. 11-6). Uncut tracks can be added to cut tracks by simply plugging in the right connectors. But cuts must be straight. A miter box will be helpful in making straight cuts.

Installing a modern track lighting system in your home is easier than you might think. In a few hours you should be able to attach the track and hook up electrical connections.

As with all home remodeling projects, you should have a clear plan drawn out on paper before you attempt the installation. One very important initial consideration is where the electrical hookup will be; that is, where the track will connect up with the house circuit. Some tracks can be connected only at the *end* of the track; others can have electrical hookups *anywhere* along the track.

The most common electrical hookup is at the end of the track (Fig. 11-7). Wires from a standard on/off switch are brought down through an outlet box in the ceiling (or wall) where you want to start

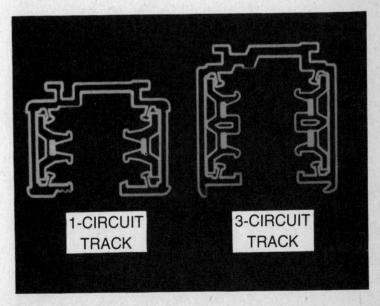

Fig. 11-5. The circuitry of a one-circuit track and a three-circuit track.

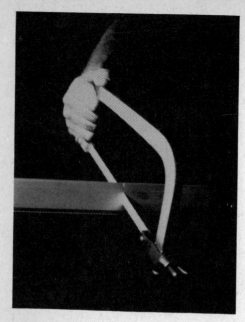

Fig. 11-6. Cutting track with a hacksaw.

your run of track. There is generally a hole in the top of the track for bringing the wires in. Usually the electrical hookup is in a "live end," which is an end cap for the track. Once the wires are connected to the live end, it is inserted into the end of the track (Fig. 11-8). The other end of the track receives a similar end cap, commonly called

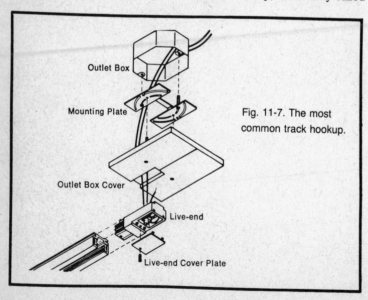

Outlet Box

Mounting Plate

Fig. 11-7. The most common track hookup.

Outlet Box Cover

Live-end

Live-end Cover Plate

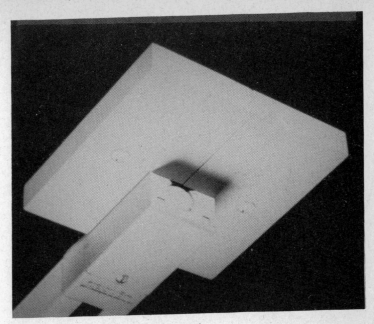

Fig. 11-8. The live end slips into the track.

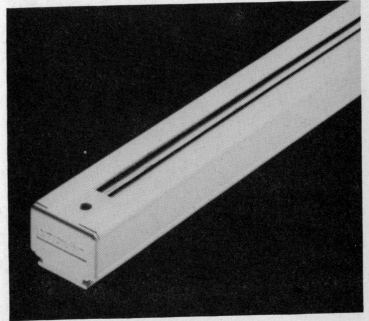

Fig. 11-9. A dead end finishes off the end of the track.

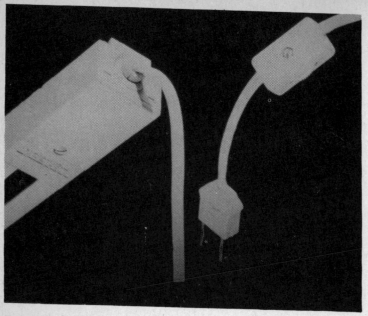

Fig. 11-10. A cord-and-plug connector.

the "dead end" (Fig. 11-9). The dead end covers the ends of the copper conductor wires.

Although direct wiring is really the most satisfactory way of wiring your track lighting system, you can use a cord-and-plug connector with some systems (Fig. 11-10). This is a live end that usually has a 15-foot cord that plugs into any electrical wall outlet. Most people prefer direct wiring to using cord-and-plug connectors because all wiring is concealed with a live-end connector. However, cord-and-plug connectors can be handy for people who are renting and may not be able to make many wiring changes.

When working with a cord-and-plug connector, *never* plug it into an electrical outlet until you have inserted it permanently into the track. And if it's necessary to remove it from the track, *first* unplug the cord from the electrical outlet.

Cord-and-plug fixtures are just *one* kind of connector; there are lots of other types around. They allow you to join tracks in hundreds of useful ways.

The better quality straight connectors are virtually invisible when used to connect two straight pieces of track (Fig. 11-11). Most track lighting manufacturers offer L-connectors which will join two sections of track at right angles (Fig. 11-12). The two sections of

Fig. 11-11. A straight connector.

Fig. 11-12. An L-connector.

Fig. 11-13. A T-connector.

Fig. 11-14. An X-connector.

148

track can be the same length or they can be different lengths. T-connectors let you join three sections of track in a T-formation (Fig. 11-13). Some manufacturers also offer an X-connector, which enables you to run track in four directions from one feed point (Fig. 11-14).

One company, Lightcraft Trackline, makes three unconventional connectors. One of them is a two-way connector with "arms" that pivot on an adjustable joint (Fig. 11-15). You can install your track at unique angles with this connector. It is even possible to create a polygon pattern by connecting a series of short pieces of track with several two-way rotating connectors. A track configuration can be planned to follow the line of a bow window or circular hallway.

Another unconventional connector is the three-way rotating type. It joins three sections of track in a radiating pattern. Arms can be rotated up to 180° to cover whatever random area you desire.

The third unconventional connector is a six-way fixture (Fig. 11-16). Located at the center of a large room, this connector can transmit electrical power in six directions to provide you with all the variables in lighting you will ever need. Like the conventional con-

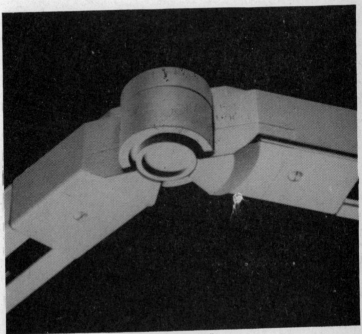

Fig. 11-15. A two-way connector with "arms."

nectors, these three connectors are available for both one- and three-circuit systems.

To install most types of track lighting systems, you must first snap a chalk line across the area. The track will be fastened along this line. The most common way of attaching the track is with toggle bolts. Usually these bolts come with the track system; if not, they can be purchased at any hardware store. Holes are drilled at predetermined intervals along the chalk line, and then the toggle bolts are used to fasten the track to the ceiling.

If your ceiling is uneven, it may be necessary to first fasten spacer clips to the ceiling (Fig. 11-17). After the clips have been installed, the track can be snapped into position.

If track lighting is to be installed to a suspended ceiling, special fasteners will be required. Some companies offer a unique clip that attaches to the tees that hold the ceiling panels in place. After these clips are in position, the track is snapped into place.

If you have a room with high ceilings, you may want to bring the track down to a lower level. Some companies offer extenders—up to 4 feet long—that are attached to the ceiling. The track is then attached to the extenders.

Fig. 11-16. A six-way connector.

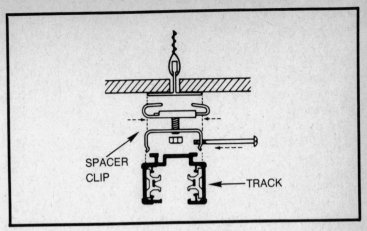

Fig. 11-17. Cross section of a spacer chip and track.

After the track has been installed and live-wired, you need only position the lights for the desired effect. With all the different lamps, holders, track connectors, and circuits, the possibilities are endless.

Chapter 12
Skylights

More light in your house doesn't have to mean bigger electric bills. It's possible to save on electricity and at the same time increase the amount of light you use each day. It's a simple matter of installing skylights. Most homes are not designed to take full advantage of the natural light surrounding them. In most cases, the installation of a skylight will provide needed light from the sun—at no additional cost.

TYPES OF SKYLIGHTS

Skylights actually provide more light than windows. Tests have shown that a skylight 2 by 3 feet will provide five times more light than a wall window of the same dimensions.

Readymade skylights are available from most lumberyards and home improvement centers (Fig. 12-1). These prefabricated skylights are easily and quickly installed by a roofer, carpenter, or skilled homeowner on any roof, pitched or flat. They are lightweight and can be easily handled by one person. Installation of a prefabricated skylight can usually be completed within a day.

Prefabricated skylights are the best bet for carefree maintenance. Frames are made of corrosion-resistant aluminum, and the window itself is, in most cases, made from acrylic plastic. This type of plastic is noted for its extraordinary strength, durability, and optical clarity. It is shatter resistant and cannot be discolored or softened by the sun's rays. It maintains its crystal clarity for life and

Fig. 12-1. Two prefabricated skylights.

is 8 to 10 times safer and more resistant to breakage than window glass. Another exciting feature about acrylic plastic skylights is that they can be molded into dome or bubble shapes, which will cause rain water to run off quickly.

There are three basic colors of acrylic skylights: clear colorless for a maximum amount of light and visibility, white translucent for evenly diffused and balanced daylighting, and tinted clear. Tinted acrylic skylights are either amber or smoke (gray) and help take the sharpness out of the sun's rays.

There are several companies that manufacture skylights for residential and commercial use. Although shapes may differ from dome to square and flat, all manufactured skylights are installed in very much the same manner. There are two basic types of installation: (1) over a wooden frame built on the roof, and (2) directly on the roof. If a wooden frame is used, all the flashing and water protection must be built around the skylight. But with skylights that are installed *directly on* the roof, all necessary weather and moisture protections are built into the skylight frame. Since a skylight with a pre-flashed aluminum curb is the easiest to install, most of the rest of this chapter will be devoted to this type.

INITIAL CONSIDERATIONS

The following six points should be considered *before* you shop for a skylight.

1. Decide on the shape of the skylight, keeping in mind that a dome-shaped skylight can be used on both a flat and pitched roof, but a flat or dormer skylight can be used only on a pitched roof.
2. Determine the color of the skylight. Remember that the type of light that comes into your home will have a bearing on atmosphere, privacy, and heat.
3. Determine whether a double or single skylight is required. Double skylights consist of outer and inner sections sepa-

rated by a sealed air space. Double skylights conserve energy by reducing heat loss in winder and heat gain in the summer. They are strongly recommended for most residential applications.

4. Determine whether you want a fixed or ventilating skylight.

5. After you determine the type and color of skylight you want, determine the size of the unit that would best suit your needs. Table 12-1 may help you decide.

6. Determine if a well or light shaft has to be built between the skylight and the room.

After you consider the above, you can begin the actual planning of the skylight installation. If you are not familiar with general roofing practices (shingling, etc.), you should do some research into how roofs are attached to houses. Though this information is not essential for installing a skylight, some background will prove invaluable when the work actually begins.

INSTALLATION

Because individual roofs and interior ceilings may require special tailoring, it is not possible to give more than generalized instructions for installing a prefabricated skylight. Some things will remain the same, however, regardless of the type of roof you are working on. Keep in mind though that building codes and building practices do differ in various parts of the country.

Your first step in installing a prefabricated skylight is to make an opening in your ceiling. This will usually entail removing some interior ceiling covering. And you must expose the roof rafters, for it is on these that the skylight will be attached.

Table 12-1. Skylights Common Sizes and Approximate Illumination.

Skylights Common Sizes and Approximate Illumination	
ROUGH OPENING (Inches)	FLOOR AREA ILLUMINATED (Square Feet)
14 × 22	up to 40
22 × 22	40 – 80
22 × 30	80 – 120
30 × 30	120 – 200
46 × 30	200– 300

In some cases, there will be an attic separating a room from the roof rafters. If this is the case, you have two choices as to how you can do the work. You can work from the attic (where the roof rafters are exposed), install the skylight, open up the interior ceiling, build a light shaft to contain the new light, and then insulate the house from the attic space. Or, you can open up the interior ceiling first, open up the roof, install the skylight, and then build the light shaft. Usually I prefer to start work in the attic. Then after the skylight has been installed, I open up the interior ceiling.

By working from the attic, you protect the interior of the house from accidental dropping of debris and the weather. Your household will be less disturbed, especially if the job runs longer than the normal one day.

When you decide where to install the skylight (i.e., between which rafters), mark this location on the outside of the roof. This is most easily accomplished by driving four eightpenny common nails, one at each corner, from the inside of the roof to the outside.

Then climb up on the roof and locate the four nails. With a shingle bar or other suitable tool, carefully remove the shingles from the area between the four nails. Begin removing the shingles at least 12 inches above the top line of the skylight location. Save as many of the shingles as you can, for you will need to replace shingles around the skylight after it has been installed. Remove at least 12 inches of the shingles from around all sides of the location of the skylight.

Next, mark the location of the skylight on the roof sheeting. Use the four nails as a guide. Cut through the roof into the attic or room below. This hole is called the *rough opening*, and on top of it the new skylight will be installed.

The easiest way to cut through a roof is with a hand held electric circular saw, using the plunge cut method. With this method, the area to be cut is marked with a heavy line. Then, the saw is held firmly and, with the protective cover for the blade held out of the way, the saw is eased down until the moving blade makes contact with the roof. Constant downward pressure is applied until the blade cuts through the roof sheeting. Then the saw can be used in the regular fashion to cut along the marked line. The same procedure is followed for each of the four lines. When all four cuts have been made, the cutout area will fall into the attic below. If it doesn't, a tap with a hammer will usually be all that is necessary to cause the cut section to fall.

Check the dimensions of the rough opening to insure they are the same as the dimensions of the skylight you will be installing. Then install headers between the rafters (Fig. 12-2).

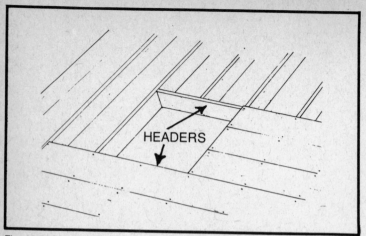

Fig. 12-2. A rough opening in a roof for skylight installation.

After the rough opening has been "framed" with the same size dimensional lumber as the rafters, apply an extra layer of roofing felt up to the edge of the rough opening (Fig. 12-3A). Fasten the felt down with staples, then seal the edges of the felt with roofing tar or roofing cement. Next, replace the roofing shingles up to the bottom edge of the opening (Fig. 12-3B). Run a band of tar around the edge of the rough opening (Fig. 12-3C). This will help to seal the edges of

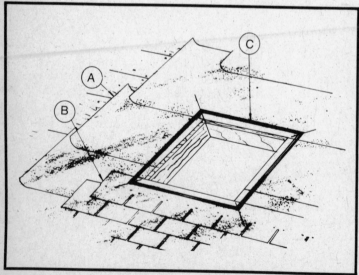

Fig. 12-3. Roof opening with felt and tiles in place.

the skylight once it has been installed. A 2-inch-wide band of roofing cement, spaced approximately 2 inches from the edge of the rough opening, will be enough. All four sides of the opening should have the cement, but it should not be put on too thickly or it will ooze into the opening after the skylight is installed.

Set the skylight into place over the rough opening and on top of the band of roofing cement. Once you have centered the skylight over the opening, you can nail down the edges of the skylight.

Drive nails approximately 1/2 inch in from the outside edge of the skylight's nailing flange; space the nails 3 inches apart (Fig. 12-4A). The nails should be driven through the flange, roof, and into the rafters below. Use 1 1/2- to 2-inch aluminum shingle nails. Next, apply a layer of roofing cement over the nailheads and nailing flange, extending the layer onto the roof 1 inch all around the opening. All four sides of the skylight should receive a coat of the cement as added protection against incoming water.

Re-install the roofing shingles around three sides of the skylight (Fig. 12-4B). Begin working at the down roof side of the skylight and continue installing the shingles until you have completed the job. On the bottom side of the skylight, nail the shingles *over* the flange (Fig. 12-4C). Put a dab of roofing cement over every exposed nailhead.

Once roofing cement has been applied to the last exposed nailhead, the outside work is completed, and the next step is to work on the interior.

If an attic separates the roof from an interior room it will be necessary to build a well, or lightshaft, to permit the skylight to shed

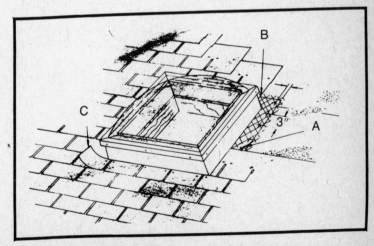

Fig. 12-4. The skylight installed.

Fig. 12-5. A lightshaft.

light into that room. A lightshaft is required only when the skylight is used in a home which has an open space between the roof and interior ceiling. The lightshaft may be boxed in with plywood, Sheetrock, redwood, tongue-and-groove boards, exterior siding, etc. It can even be painted white to reflect daylight into the room, or the shaft may be painted to blend with the room ceiling or wall color. A translucent panel may also be used to finish off the ceiling openings.

In most installation where a lightshaft is required, it will be possible to design it so the opening at the roof will be directly above the opening at the ceiling. This condition will be true for both pitched and flat roofs.

In some installations of skylights, it will be desirable to make the ceiling opening larger than the roof opening to spread the daylight over a wider area. In some instances, the lightshaft may be easily extended at its base. This may be done whether the roof is flat or pitched.

Figure 12-5 shows basically what is involved in building a lightshaft. The shaft is built between the roofing rafters and the ceiling joists. Once the shaft has been framed out, the interior can be covered, as noted above, with suitable materials.

Chapter 13
Thermal Insulation

In the good old days—about 10 years ago—when energy was a lot cheaper, home insulation didn't mean much. It was the stuff contractors crammed between the ceiling joists—sometimes. And after all, who worried then about losing energy through the walls? If you got the shivers, you turned up the thermostat. But as fuel costs go up, the importance of effective thermal insulation increases. So today insulation gets a lot more respect from homeowner and builder alike. We know now that it can effectively reduce heating costs in the winter and take big bites out of electric bills in the summer. And a lot of people are finding out that good insulation can also help maintain comfortable, uniform temperatures throughout the house—no more cold floors, no more chilly drafts.

It makes little sense to insulate just your floors and ceilings while ignoring other vulnerable areas in your house—like your walls, your crawl space, etc. So this chapter will cover *all* the bases: It'll tell you how to install insulation anywhere in your house, particularly the places that need insulation the most.

HEAT TRANSFER

Stop heat transfer in your house and you save energy—and money. The whole idea of insulation is to prevent heat from seeping *out* of your house in winter and *into* your house in summer.

Unfortunately, heat can move about (can be transferred) in more than one way. In general, anytime there's a temperature

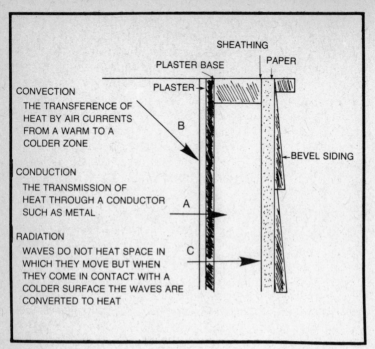

Fig. 13-1. The three methods of heat transfer.

difference, heat flows. And one way it flows is by *conduction*: Heat can travel (be conducted) from one molecule to the next. If you stick a lit candle under one end of a steel rod, heat will soon be conducted through the metal to the other end. The same goes for walls, floors, and ceilings: If they're uninsulated, heat can move through them at surprising rates (Fig. 13-1A). But the good news is that different materials have different rates of conduction. That steel rod, for instance, can transfer heat a lot faster than a wooden pole. And (thank goodness) thermal insulation transmits heat much more slowly than wall studs, siding, and masonry.

Then there's *convection*, the transfer of heat by actual motion of the hot material (usually air). In an uninsulated house, convection works something like this: Since the density of air decreases as temperature increases, warm air from a heat source (a furnace, say) rises. But cool, heavier air coming through the uninsulated floor, walls, and ceiling sinks, pushing the warm air aside, setting up continual air (convection) currents. Needless to say, all those swirling eddies can make a house pretty uncomfortable. Convection currents can flow any place where there is both warm and cool air, even inside walls (Fig. 13-1B).

Heat can also be transmitted by *radiation*; that is, in radiant waves of energy. When heat radiates from a source, like the sun, it traverses space and warms only the surface that it strikes. It travels in straight lines, from source to receptive surface, always from a warmer surface to a cooler one. If you own a fireplace, you know a little something about radiant heat: The heat from the flames can be radiated across the room, warming the front of you, leaving a chill on your back. As Fig. 13-1C shows, heat can be radiated through the space in uninsulated walls. But radiant heat can be deflected just as light can; a sheet of aluminum foil or other reflective material on the cooler wall could actually reduce heat buildup.

HOW INSULATION WORKS

So the job of *any* insulation is to retard heat transfer, to prevent heat from passing through your walls, floor, and ceiling. Sounds simple enough. But if you look closer, things get more complicated. First of all, some materials are good insulators; some are not. And that means that even store-bought insulating materials vary in their ability to keep a house snug in winter. What's more, you can't always judge insulation by its thickness. A 1-inch-thick piece of fiberglass, for example, can insulate *better* than a 1-foot-thick concrete wall.

Climate is a factor too. If you live in a cold-winter region or in an area of sky-high fuel costs, you'll need a lot more insulation than folks in other parts of the country. Then there's another kink in the fabric: When it comes to installing insulation, there's always a point of diminishing returns. If you slap some insulation in an uninsulated wall, you're going to drastically cut that wall's heat loss, maybe by as much as 50%. If you double that insulation, your total reduction in heat loss will *not* double also—it will simply increase slightly. Fact is, the more insulation you add, the less effect it will have on the *total decrease* in heat loss. After a while, the costs of insulating outweigh the benefits.

Fortunately, there's an easy way to sort out all these complications. The conducting or insulating properties of any material can be described by heat-loss coefficients, or factors. Using these factors, you can intelligently compare insulating materials on the basis of their effectiveness in reducing heat transfer—not on the basis of thickness, cost, or salesmen's claims. You can then determine exactly how much insulation you need.

One important factor is *thermal conductivity*, or k. The k factor tells you how much heat (in BTUs) can pass through 1 square foot of homogeneous material 1 inch thick in 1 hour when there is a 1° F

Table 13-1. K Factors for Common Building Materials (1 Square Foot In Area).

MATERIAL	THICKNESS	K FACTOR
cork board	1"	0.27
fiberglass	1"	0.27
glass foam	1"	0.40
polystyrene foam	1"	0.15
rock wool	1"	0.29
fir	1"	0.67
pine, soft	1"	0.86
particle board	1"	0.50
sawdust	1"	0.41
brick, face	1"	10.00
brick, common	1"	5.00
gypsum wall board	1"	0.70
stone	8"	0.70
stone	12"	0.50
cinder block	8"	0.50
	12"	0.35
concrete, block	8"	0.55
	12"	0.45
concrete poured	8"	0.70
	12"	0.50

difference between the two surfaces. (A BTU, or British thermal unit, is a standard measure of heat energy; 1 BTU is the amount of heat needed to raise the temperature of 1 pound of water by 1° F.) The important thing to remember is that the lower the k factor, the better the insulating ability of the material.

Take a look at Table 13-1. The k factor for a 1-inch-thick piece of cork board is 0.27. That means that 0.27 BTUs can pass through that cork board every hour (if there's a 1° F temperature difference). The k factor for a 1-inch-thick piece of gypsum wallboard, however, is 0.70. Such a comparison leads us to a very helpful conclusion: Cork board is more than twice as good an insulator as gypsum board. So if you know the k factor of a given insulating material, you really know a great deal about that material's heat-stopping capability.

Another important factor is *thermal conductivity for walls,* or U. The k factor tells you about the conducting capabilities of *specific* materials; the U factor gives you the same information—about *whole* walls. So the U factor is the amount of heat (in BTUs) that passes through a *building section* in 1 hour when there is a 1° F difference between the inside and outside temperatures.

How do you find U factors for specific kinds of walls? Call your local heating contractor or utility company. They'll usually have charts and tables that list the U factors for just about any type of wall you can think of. And that kind of information is pretty valuable. You can learn what effect added insulation can have on certain walls, how much heat you can save by adding aluminum siding, and what types of walls do the best job of keeping the winter out.

By far the most useful factor is *resistance*, or R. The R factor is a measure of a material's resistance to heat flow; thus, the higher the R value, the more effective the material is as an insulator. Thermal insulation is rated according to R factor, so packages or rolls of insulation are marked with R numbers. R11 insulation is clearly a better heat stopper than R7 insulation, and a layer of R7 over a layer of R11 equals a blanket of insulation with R18 rating. The R factors of some common insulating materials are shown in Table 13-2.

So when you're shopping around for insulation, check the R numbers closely. Never mind the thickness of the material. Never mind the *species* of the material. The R factor tells the tale.

The U factor and the R factor are related by this formula:

$$U = \frac{R}{1}$$

Thus the U value of a construction section (a wall, for example) is the reciprocal of the R value of that section (or of the combined R *values* of the individual materials in the section). You can see then that beefing up the insulation (increasing the R value) reduces the heat

Table 13-2. R Factors for Common Insulating Materials.

MATERIAL	THICKNESS	R FACTOR
insulation, spun rock or fiberglass	2"	7
	3 – 4"	11 – 14
	5 – 8"	19 – 22
plywood	3⁄8"	0.47
	1⁄2"	0.62
	5⁄8"	0.78
	3⁄4"	0.94
brick, common	1"	0.20
brick, face	1"	0.11
gypsum wall board	1"	0.90
pine, soft	1"	1.20
shingles, asphalt		0.44
shingles, wood		0.94

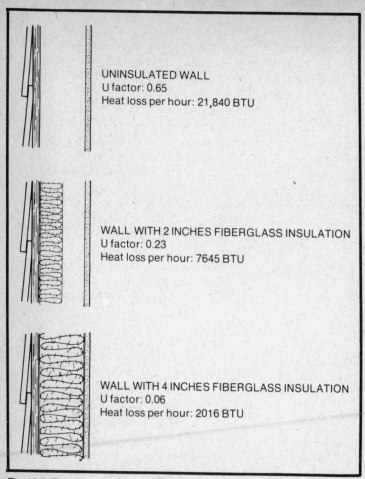

UNINSULATED WALL
U factor: 0.65
Heat loss per hour: 21,840 BTU

WALL WITH 2 INCHES FIBERGLASS INSULATION
U factor: 0.23
Heat loss per hour: 7645 BTU

WALL WITH 4 INCHES FIBERGLASS INSULATION
U factor: 0.06
Heat loss per hour: 2016 BTU

Fig. 13-2. This demonstrates the difference insulation can make in a typical wall. The effects of adding insulation are magnified a little, since we ignored the insulating effects of the air film on each side of the wall. But in most cases, four inches of insulation will reduce the heat loss by 75 to 80 percent.

flow (decreases the U value). So if you add some R7 insulation to a typical wood-frame wall that has a U value of 0.22, you can cut the wall's U factor down to 0.10. If you stuff some R11 insulation into that wall, you can knock the U value down to 0.07, which is about average for residential exterior walls.

Now let's take a look at what good insulation means in dollars and cents. Let's say your house has an uninsulated wall with a U factor of 0.65. If the wall has an area of 480 square feet and there's a temperature difference (between the inside and outside of the house) of 70° F, your house will lose 21,840 BTUs per hour (Fig. 13-2). Just through the wall alone! And if your power company charges you $0.026 for every kilowatt you use, that leaky wall will cost you $0.17 per hour. That's $4.08 per day! And in a year...Don't even think about it. But if you add 2 inches of fiberglass insulation to that wall, your heat loss will be only 7645 BTUs per hour. Or about $0.058 per hour. Add 2 more inches and you'll reduce the heat loss to 2016 BTUs per hour. And that translates to $0.36 per day! Thus just 4 inches of fiberglass insulation can make a wall 10 times tighter—and 10 times less painful to the pocketbook.

INSULATING MATERIALS

Insulating materials can be grouped into five categories: (1) flexible, (2) rigid, (3) reflective, (4) loose-fill, and (5) miscellaneous types.

Flexible insulation comes in two forms, blanket and batt. The blanket type is probably the one you're most familiar with. It's manufactured in strips or rolls—usually just wide enough to fit between joists or studs with standard spacing (16 or 24 inches). Standard thicknesses are 1 1/2, 2, and 3 inches (Fig. 13-3A).

Batt insulation comes in rectangular sections—generally 4 or 6 inches thick, 15 or 23 inches wide, and 24 or 48 inches long (Fig. 13-3B). Batt is a little harder to install than blanket, but inch for inch their insulating power is about the same.

Blanket and batt insulation are both made out of the same stuff—mineral or vegetable fibers. A popular insulating mineral fiber is rock wool, a kind of shredded limestone or slag. Fiberglass is another heat-retarding mineral fiber, created by spinning molten glass into thin strands. The vegetable (or organic) fibers are usually concocted out of wood or cotton—and because these materials have food value, they're treated to make them verminproof, decayproof, and insectproof. And federal laws require that they be fire resistant.

Unfortunately, many flexible insulations can irritate your skin. So never touch them bare-handed; always wear gloves.

Most flexible insulation has some kind of backing—on just one side of the material, or on both. Usually if there are two backings, one will be a vapor barrier, a thin-skinned defense against moisture that can creep through floors, ceilings, and walls. Regular backings are nearly always paper; vapor-barrier backings are either plastic, foil, or asphalt. And for the convenience of people who don't want to spend a lifetime putting in insulation, most backings have fastening tabs on the sides. Just press the insulation in place and staple the tabs

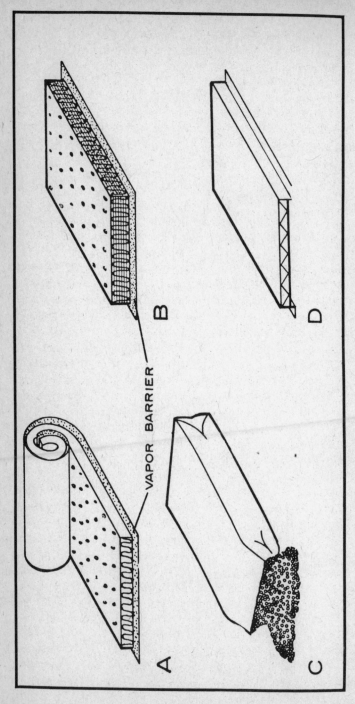

VAPOR BARRIER

Fig. 13-3. Four types of thermal insulation: (A) blanket, (B) batt, (C) loose fill, and (D) reflective.

166

to the studs or joists; the insulation will stay put forever. Tabless insulation, however, is available too. Most of it is the friction-fit type: Wedge it between studs or joists and it stays, without staples, without nails.

Rigid insulation is either structural or nonsturctural. The nonstructural stuff is strictly for insulating, not for building—and that means it is usually lighter, weaker, and flimsier than structural heat-stoppers. Conventional wallboard, some building boards, most sheathing, and all roof decking are structural building/insulating materials.

If you shop for rigid insulation, you're going to run smack into a thoroughly disconcerting variety of sizes and materials. This brand of house-warmer is made out of processed wood, sugarcane, polystyrene, polyurethane, cork, mineral wool, and a whole array of vegetable fibers. All rigid insulation comes in some kind of board form, but the sizes vary greatly—from 12-inch squares to boards 4 feet wide, 12 feet long, and 1 inch thick. You can buy the structural types in sheets—2 by 8 feet, 4 by 8 feet, and 4 by 12 feet.

Now about polystyrene and polyurethane boards. They make fantastic rigid insulators, insulators which have closed-cell constructions that won't pass air or hold water. They're lightweight, insectproof, and odorproof. Better still, they have superlow k factors—from 0.15 to 0.25 per inch of thickness. That's an R factor of about 4 to 7 per inch thickness. You can cut these boards into virtually any shape, wedge them between joists and studs, glue them to cement walls, even use them as a base for cement foundations.

However, they have one big drawback. They burn. They are not easily inflamed, but they *will burn*—and give off toxic fumes. So if you favor this kind of insulation, install it *inside* your walls, floor, and ceiling—*never outside*.

Reflective insulations are comparatively lightweight, sometimes paper thin, and always shiny, shiny enough to deflect radiated heat the way a mirror deflects light (Fig. 13-3D). Thus most of these insulations are plain old aluminum foil, tin-coated sheet metal, or paper covered with reflective oxide. You can use them to keep heat in the house in the winter—or to deflect the sun's warmth in the summer. However, reflective materials probably work best as a shield against *external* radiated heat, against the radiant warmth that beats down from the sun and permeates your walls and ceiling.

In order for reflective insulation to do its job, there must be an air space in front of the reflective surface, normally at least 3/4 inch deep, 1 1/2 inches deep for ceilings. If the reflective surface butts against some other material, the insulation is worthless. Perhaps

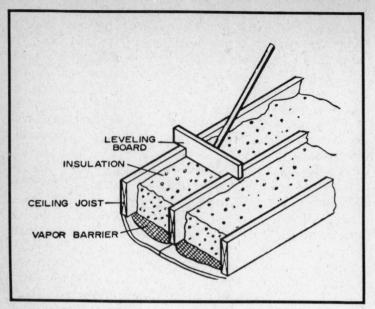

LEVELING BOARD

INSULATION

CEILING JOIST

VAPOR BARRIER

Fig. 13-4. Loose-fill insulation is poured into place and raked level.

even worse than worthless: It can then become a superconductor of heat!

Probably the most efficient reflective insulation is the accordion type—made up of several layers of foil separated by spacers. This stuff comes in rolls and can be stapled between studs and joists. And—like most reflective heat-stoppers—it can also be attached directly to blanket insulation or the stud side of gypsum board.

Loose-fill insulation is granular, consisting of small bits of material that can be poured, blown, or hand-raked into wall cavities or between ceiling joists (Fig. 13-3C). The granular fill is usually shredded bark, sawdust, vermiculite, chopped rock wool, wood shavings, chopped fiberglass, or bits of cork.

The good news is the ease of installation. You can pour loose fill into a wall cavity from above—from the attic. Or you can have it blown into your walls through small holes. If you've got a ceiling to insulate, you can rake loose fill between the attic joists (Fig. 13-4). No stapling. No gluing. And no ripping out wall panels.

Like most kinds of insulation, loose fill is insectproof and fireproof. But it has disadvantages too. It will settle in time, reducing air space between particles, lowering the insulating value. But a bigger problem is insulation "dust," the tiny particles that pervade the air during the installation of rock wool and fiberglass loose fill. This dust, if inhaled, may harm you. And, according to the Consumer Product Safety Commission, fiberglass dust is especially suspect. Loose-fill materials may also irritate your skin. So to be on the safe side when handling loose fill, wear thick clothing, gloves, and some kind of mouth-nose mask.

Now the miscellaneous category. First, there're the sprayed insulations, the inorganic fibrous materials—usually rock wool or fiberglass—that can be blown into your walls or attic. An insulation contractor has to handle this kind of installation, but his charge for blasting the stuff into place will generally be comparable to the cost of other professionally installed insulations. Next: foamed-in-place insulation. This type is becoming increasingly popular. (These days it's hard to miss a hard-sell TV commercial hawking this stuff.) Installation is the epitome of technical simplicity: The contractor drills a few inconspicuous holes in your walls, snakes in a flexible tube, and floods the cavities with insulating foam—either polystyrene or urethane. The foam hardens and your walls are ready to keep out the cold. The advantage of this kind of installation—and spray-in techniques too—is that already-built homes can be fully insulated without a lot of expensive wall wrecking.

Table 13-3 will help you compare the heat-stopping capabilities of various types of insulation. Remember, the k factor is the recip-

Table 13-3. Thermal Conductivity Values of Insulating Materials.

Insulation group		"k" range (Conductivity)
General	Specific type	
Flexible Fill	Standard materials Vermiculite	0.25 – 0.27 .28 – .30 .45 – .48
Reflective (2 sides)		(1)
Rigid	Insulating fiberboard Sheathing fiberboard	.35 – .36 .42 – .55
Foam	Polystyrene Urethane	.25 – .29 .15 – .17
Wood	Low density	.60 – .65

(1) Insulating value is equal to slightly more than 1 inch of flexible insulation. (Resistance, "R = 4.3).

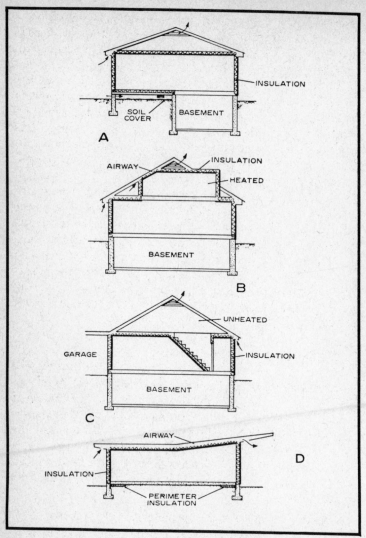

Fig. 13-5. Use insulation to separate heated areas from unheated areas.

rocal of the R factor. Thus, a k value of 0.25 is equal to an R value of 1/0.25, or 4.0.

WHERE TO INSULATE

No use insulating every square inch of your house. Just insulate where it really counts. Follow this rule: Insulate any barrier (wall, ceiling, floor, roof, etc.) that separates heated space from unheated space. That means you should install insulation in all exterior walls and the ceiling (Fig. 13-5A). If your house has a crawl space, insulate the floor or foundation. Unless you're planning on turning the basement into a rec room, you can forget about insulating the basement walls. However, if your attic is unheated, you certainly can't forget about that. Seal it off from the rest of the house: Insulate around the attic stairway and be sure to weatherstrip the attic door (Fig. 13-5C) The same insulating rule applies to 1 1/2-story houses: Install insulation between the warm and the cool—even if the cool happens to be a behind-the-wall attic-like area (Fig. 13-5B). Insulate around dormers, bay windows, and stairways.

Did you notice the little arrows in Fig. 13-5? They're reminders that houses—especially insulated ones—have to be ventilated topside. Attics without vents can trap a lot of heat in the summer, and that heat can be transmitted through the ceiling to the rooms below. If the blistering sun heats up your unvented attic to 150°F (and it can happen!), you won't be able to keep *any* room cool, no matter how much insulation you install. So wherever you insulate, make sure you don't block any air vents—and if there aren't any vents, make some.

You have to be especially careful when insulating the ceiling of a house with a flat or low-pitched roof. Ceiling insulation in these structures must allow air to circulate along the length of the joists. That is, there must be airways for ventilation (Fig. 13-5D).

Should you insulate unheated garages and workshops? It depends. If these structures adjoin the house, insulation can keep them warmer in the winter because they'll trap some of the heat that seeps through the house walls. If they're not attached to the house, forget the insulation. Of course, even a partially heated outbuilding should have insulation—in the ceiling, in the walls, and (if possible) under the foundation.

Here's a simple test you can perform to determine whether an exterior house wall has adequate insulation. On a cool day, with an outdoor temperature at least 20°F less than the indoor temperature, attach a thermometer to an interior (partition) wall. After a few minutes note the reading. Then move the thermometer across the room to an exterior wall. Attach it; wait; take a reading. If the temperature difference is more than 1.5°F for each 10°F of indoor/outdoor temperature difference, the exterior wall needs more insulation. Let's say the outdoor temperature is 30°F. And let's assume you get a reading of 70°F on an interior wall. That means the indoor/outdoor temperature difference is 40°F. If the reading on an

Table 13-4. Comparative Cost Summary of Creating a Heated Crawl Space vs Installing Floor Insulation.

Item	Quantity	Installed Unit Cost	Foundation Wall Insulation	Floor Insulation
Floor Insulation – R11 Reverse Flange [1]	1500 SF	$0.17/SF		$255.00
Foundation Wall Insulation – R11 Blanket [2]	400 SF	$0.14/SF	$ 56.00	
Vapor Barrier – 4 mil Polyethylene	1500 SF	$32.00/MSF	$ 48.00	
Foundation Vents – 12"x24" Screen / 8"x16" Operable Louvres	8 / 2	$6.50/Ea / $8.75/Ea	$ 17.50	$ 52.00
Heating Duct Insulation – 2" Flexible Wrap	264 SF	$0.55/SF		$145.20
Water Pipe Insulation – 1" Thick	50 LF	$1.75/LF		$ 87.50
			$121.50	$539.70 −121.50
		COST DIFFERENCE		$418.20

(1) If supporting wire is required, add $0.05/SF.

(2) If 1" polystyrene insulation is used, substitute $0.25/SF.

exterior wall (within the same room) is less than 64°F, the insulation in that wall is inadequate.

INSULATING A CRAWL SPACE

If your house has a crawl space, you've got two options. To cut the flow of heat through your floors, you can (1) insulate the floor itself or (2) create a heated crawl space (that is, insulate the crawl-space walls and cover the ground with a vapor barrier). The use of either technique can help keep your floors warm in winter, but the second option is easier on the budget.

Table 13-4 is a comparison of the two techniques; the figures are based on a typical house measuring 30 by 50 feet. Insulating the floor costs $539.70: $255.00 for 1500 square feet of insulation for the floor joists; $52.00 for foundation vents; and $232.70 for pipe and duct insulation. On the other hand, the cost of insulating the crawl space is only $121.50; $56.00 for 400 square feet of insulation for the crawl-space (foundation) wall; $48.00 for a vapor barrier; and $17.50 for foundation vents. The saving is over $400! Why the cost difference? Well, for one thing, an insulated crawl space captures a lot of heat from above and is thus a *heated* crawl space: underfloor pipes and vents don't have to be insulated. And since an insulated crawl space has a vapor barrier, fewer foundation vents are needed.

So to make a *heated* crawl space, you have to have insulated foundation walls: keeps out the cold; keeps in the heat. You need a vapor barrier too: It seals off moisture from the ground, preventing condensation on the subflooring and the insulation. And you've got to have adequate venting—most houses do—so that air can circulate and carry moisture out of the crawl space.

The biggest job is insulating the foundation walls and laying a vapor barrier. Here's the easiest way to do it:

1. Cover the crawl-space "floor" with 4- or 6-mil-thick polyethylene sheets, overlapping them at least 3 inches. Spread this vapor barrier right up to the foundation walls (Fig. 13-6).

2. Glue or nail flexible insulation to the crawl-space walls, making sure it extends over the top of the wall and down onto the vapor barrier. If the insulation has a vapor barrier of its own, face it out toward the crawl space, not toward the wall.

3. To make sure the polyethylene stays put, people usually top it with a 3-inch layer of gravel, sand, dirt, or crushed limestone. (Check with local building codes for exact requirements.) Spread the material to the edge of the wall insulation.

4. Joist headers crown foundation walls; heat can pass through them too. Insulate them with at least 4 inches of

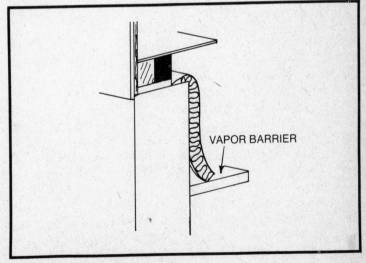

VAPOR BARRIER

Fig. 13-6. Insulating a crawl space.

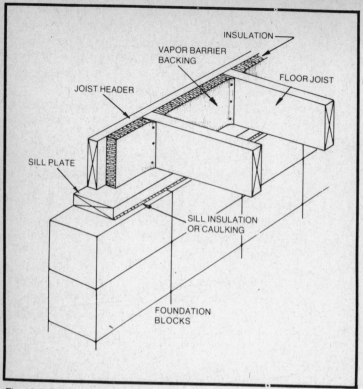

Fig. 13-7. Four inches of fiberglass insulation should be placed between the floor joists and the joist header. This insulation should have some type of vapor barrier backing, and it is installed with the backing facing toward the crawl space and tacked to the floor joists.

flexible insulation—insulation that has a vapor-barrier backing (Fig. 13-7). Tack or staple it to the floor joists, making sure the vapor barrier faces the crawl space. If you're building a house and insulating as you go, this step should be undertaken *after* you lay the subfloor.

Here's another way to insulate crawl-space walls and install a vapor barrier—a method usually employed when houses are being built. This technique involves a lot more work, but the result is generally a tighter crawl space, a warmer floor.

1. This job calls for *rigid* insulation. If you really want your money's worth, buy some first-rate polystyrene or polyurethane boards. They're good insulators, won't compress very easily, and absolutely cannot soak up water.

Plus, they do double duty: They're excellent vapor barriers.

2. You should install this insulation partially *below* crawl-space "floor" level. That means you'll have to dig a trench along the foundation wall—6 to 8 inches deep in warm climates, 14 to 18 inches elsewhere (Fig. 13-8).

3. You can either glue or nail the insulation to the foundation walls. To nail it on, first press the insulation into the trench and up against the wall, positioning the top edge of the insulation flush with the highest row of cement blocks (Fig. 13-8). Use 1- by 2-inch wooden strips as a nailing base: Position them across the face of the insulation (horizontally) and drive concrete nails through them, all the way into the blocks.

4. Backfill the trench with the dirt you removed.

5. Cover the crawl-space ground with 4- or 6-mil-thick polyethylene. Whether it comes in rolls or sheets, the sections should be overlapped at least 6 inches. Run the polyethylene up the insulation about 3 inches (Fig. 13-9).

6. Cover the vapor barrier with some kind of granular material, according to local building codes.

7. Insulate the joist headers as explained earlier.

INSULATING THE FLOOR (OVER A CRAWL SPACE)

The alternative to insulating your crawl space is insulating your floor. Sound like a big job? It's not. One hardworking do-it-yourselfer

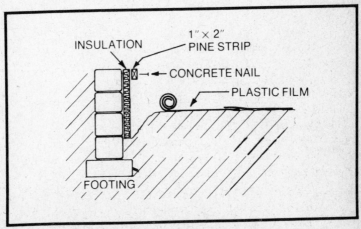

Fig. 13-8. Installing rigid insulation in the crawl space.

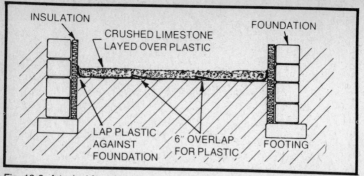

Fig. 13-9. A typical foundation is insulated with rigid insulation. A vapor barrier has been installed here using plastic sheets with their seams overlapped.

could probably insulate the floor of a 30- by 50-foot house in one afternoon. (I'm not talking about insulating heating ducts and water pipes; that's another ball game.) The task nevertheless has its vexations: you'll have to creep around in the crawl space and spend a lot of time craning your neck to fasten the insulation overhead.

Flexible insulation is best for the job. Installation is just a matter of unpacking it and securing it between the floor joists. However, there are over a half-dozen ways to do the securing. You can staple the edges of the insulation backing to the bottoms of the joists (Fig. 13-10A), or you can staple the backing edges to the *sides* of the joists (Fig. 13-10B). Either method works fine. You can also support the insulation with wood lath (Fig. 13-11). Nail the strips (usually 3/4 by 1 1/2 inch) to the bottoms of the floor joists, spacing them 24 to 36 inches apart. And if you don't feel like tracking out the lumberyard for lath, you can put the insulation up with wire. Heavy-gauge steel wire can be an installation shortcut: cut it into short pieces (slightly longer than the joist's spacing) and bow them between the joists (Fig. 13-12A). The tension on the wire will make the wire ends bite into the sides of the joists, keeping the insulation in place without staples, tacks, or lath. Of course you can also use *light* wire to support between-the-joists insulation, but it's a little more work. String the wire across the bottoms of the joists, stapling it in place as you go (Fig. 13-12B). The use of friction-fit batt insulation is another alternative, another work-saver. Just press it into place between the joists, flat against the subfloor (Fig. 13-13). To bolster the insulation's staying power, you can dab some asphalt cement on the backing before setting it into place.

If you have to cut flexible insulation, slice it with a knife. A clean, severing sweep with a sharp blade will go a long way toward keeping those skin-irritating insulation particles out of the air.

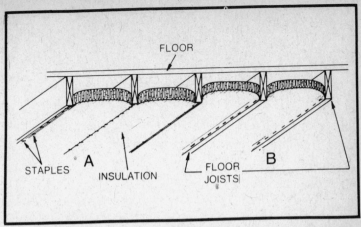

Fig. 13-10. If the insulation has a backing material, it can be stapled to the floor joists using either of the methods shown above. At the left, the backing is pulled over the bottom of the joist and stapled; while at the right, the backing is stapled to the sides of the joists. In either case, the vapor barrier must face toward the heated side of the floor.

Floor insulation should have a vapor-barrier backing. And no matter how you fasten the insulation to the joists, the vapor barrier should face the subfloor. If it doesn't, moisture will condense in the insulation, reducing the R factor to zilch. You see, when warm moist air meets cool air, condensation takes place. If the vapor barrier faces the crawl space, warm moist air from your house will permeate your floor, seep (slowly!) though the insulation, and condense on the

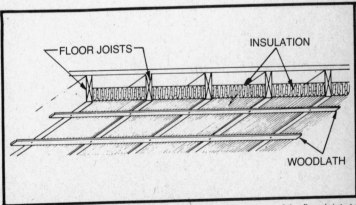

Fig. 13-11. Small wood lath strips can be nailed to the bottom of the floor joists to support the insulation. The strips are 3/4" by 1 1/2" and they are spaced 24 to 36 inches apart.

177

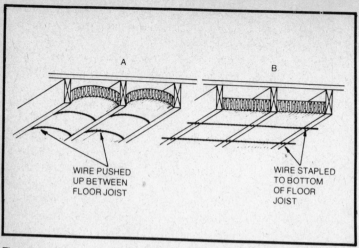

Fig. 13-12. (A) Heavy gauge steel wire is used here to support the insulation. This wire is cut long enough that it bows upward, and the ends of the wire grip the sides of the joists. (B) Light wire is held to the floor joists with staples to support the insulation.

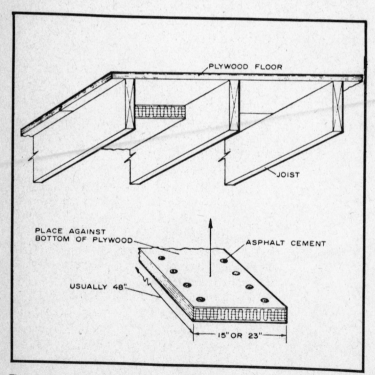

Fig. 13-13. Installing friction-fit batt between floor joists.

insulation side of the vapor barrier. Turn the insulation around so that the barrier faces the floor: Then you've stopped the moist air before it reaches cooler realms.

Just a reminder: If the insulation has a reflective backing, face the reflective surface toward the floor and leave an air space of at least 3/4 inch between the backing and floor boards.

Lately, building experts have been recommending R11 floor insulation for most houses in this country—and R19 (or better) floor insulation for houses in cold-winter states. But this isn't a rule to swear by. The amount of insulation you need in your floors depends largely on the cost of home heating in your area. The higher the cost, the more insulation you need.

If you're building a new house and insulating the frame walls as you go, you're way ahead of the game. You can insulate without having a rip out wallboard or call a contractor to blast loose fill between wall studs. You have access to every nook and cranny of the wall cavities.

INSULATING WALLS

If you're building a new house and insulating the frame walls as you go, you're way ahead of the game. You can insulate without having to rip out wallboard or call a contractor to blast loose fill between wall studs. You have access to every nook and cranny of the wall cavities.

This is how you would tackle the job:

1. This project calls for *flexible* insulation, grades R11 to R16. Whether you buy blanket or batt, make sure you get the right width for the stud spacing—15-inch width is for 16-inch stud spacing; 23-inch width fits 24-inch stud spacing.
2. Press the insulation between the wall studs, pushing until it kisses the back wall. Start at the ceiling and work your way down. Fit the insulation tightly against the studs, sole plates, and top plates—but don't squash it or it'll lose some of its insulating capability (Fig. 13-14). If the insulation has a vapor-barrier backing, face the barrier towards the inside of the house. And if there's a reflective backing, face it towards the room and make sure it'll have a 3/4-inch air space in front of it (between it and the wallboard).
3. Starting at the ceiling, staple the insulation backing (or stapling tabs) to the sides or faces of the studs, a staple every 8 inches along the stud lengths (Fig. 13-15A). Friction-fit insulation, of course, doesn't require stapling; wedge it in place and it'll stay put.

Fig. 13-14. Wedge the insulation between the studs, filling every crevice.

4. The way you finish off the insulation at the top and bottom plates is critical. All you can do with friction-fit insulation is butt it hard against these plates. But blanket and batt can sometimes be stapled or "custom cut" to fit nearly airtight (Fig. 13-16). Whatever method you use, try to get a good seal.

5. Insulate every crevice, every crack, every hole. Stuff pieces of flexible insulation around window and door frames, behind vents and pipes, in holes cut for electrical wiring and plumbing pipes.

6. If the between-the-studs insulation doesn't have a vapor barrier, install one: Cover the inside of the insulated wall(s) with 2-mil-thick polyethylene (Fig. 13-15B). First staple sheets of the stuff to the top of each insulated wall, letting them hang like curtains. Then, working from ceiling to floor, staple the sheets to the studs.

You can insulate masonry walls too, but you have to provide a base for the insulation, something that the insulation can hang on to.

1. Nail 2- by 2-inch wood strips to the masonry wall you want to insulate. Use concrete nails and attach the strips 16 or 24 inches apart, depending on the width of insulation you use (Fig. 13-17).

2. Most people use R7 flexible insulation for this project. This type is about 1 3/4 inches thick, just thick enough to neatly fill the space between strips, flush with the strip faces.

Position the insulation between the strips and staple the backing edges (or stapling tabs) to the strips. If the insulation has a vapor-barrier backing, face it toward the heated side of the wall. If there's no vapor barrier, make your own, as explained earlier.

3. If you want a finished wall, you can nail paneling or wallboard to the strips, right over the insulation. And if you prefer *more* insulation, you'll have to attach thicker strips so you can install thicker insulation.

If you've got a congenital aversion to pounding nails into masonry walls, perhaps you'll prefer the following alternative method. Using a strong waterproof adhesive, glue rigid insulation panels to your masonry walls. The lightweight polystyrene or

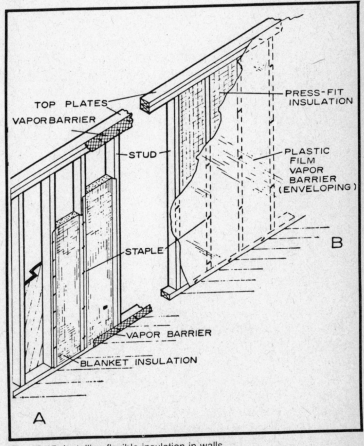

Fig. 13-15. Installing flexible insulation in walls.

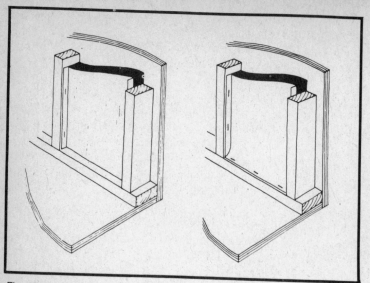

Fig. 13-16. Two ways of terminating the ends of flexible insulation.

polyurethane boards are perfect for this. And once the adhesive dries, you can glue wood paneling over the insulation.

INSULATING THE CEILING

Which kind of insulation is the most important: floor, crawl space, wall, or ceiling? There's no contest; ceiling insulation is *the* number-one structural heat-stopper in 20th-century homes. Good ceiling insulation can actually slash heating bills in half. And the reason is simple: Houses lose most of their heat energy via the ceiling—not through the windows or walls.

But how much ceiling insulation do you need? It's hard to say. Mostly because fuel prices are unstable: The value of insulation always fluctuates with fuel costs. When fuel is cheap, you don't need mounds and mounds of insulation. When fuel is not so cheap, you want to make the most out of every BTU you buy: You want insulation aplenty. But you have to look ahead too, to times when insulation may be even more important, even more valuable.

Fortunately, there are some ballpark guidelines. Houses in cold-winter states should have R30 insulation in their ceilings. Houses in other areas should have R11 to R19 ceiling insulation—that's the equivalent of 3 to 6 inches of fiberglass batt.

To get more precise information, you'll have to go to local sources—to local insulation contractors, builders, and building suppliers. Talk to people who know how the cost of energy can affect the amount of insulation you need.

Adding insulation to your ceiling (with an attic) is a fairly simple process. You can install batt, pour in loose fill, or hire a contractor to blow insulation in.

If you opt to add batt insulation, buy the kind without a backing. A backing can trap moisture in the insulation and reduce heat-stopping capability. However, if you get stuck with backed insulation, slash the backing so the moisture can escape.

Lay the batt on top of the old insulation, butting the new sections tightly together. If the old stuff fills up the space between the joists, lay the new *over* the joists, perpendicular to them (Fig. 13-18).

Some people prefer the loose fill to the batt, mostly because loose fill is easier to install. Just dump it out of the bags into the space between the joists and level it off. Instructions on the bags will tell you how deep the fill should be in order to achieve certain R factors.

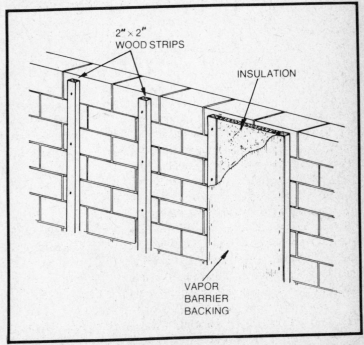

Fig. 13-17. To insulate a masonry wall, first attach wood strips to the wall using concrete nails, staple the backing of R7 insulation batting to the lath, and then cover the wall with wallboard. Use insulation with a vapor barrier backing and be sure the backing faces toward the heated living area.

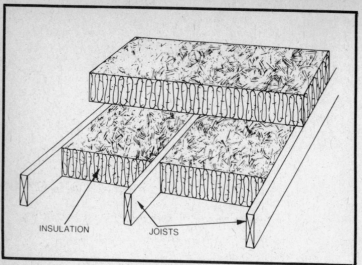

INSULATION

JOISTS

Fig. 3-18. Insulating the attic with flexible insulation.

But remember, loose fill settles, so allow for this change in depth by making the initial thickness a little "fat."

Installing insulation in an *uninsulated* attic (ceiling) is a different story: You have to consider vapor barriers. The Federal Housing Administration says that a vapor barrier in the ceiling is not necessary if there is at least 1 square foot of ceiling (attic) ventilation for every 300 square feet of attic (floor) space. The FHA also insists that half this ventilation should be at the top of the attic and half in the eaves. At any rate, you should decide whether or not you'll need a vapor barrier *before* you buy insulation. Three days after buying a truckload of backless batt is not the time to realize that you need insulation with a vapor barrier.

Wedge batt insulation between the ceiling joists, flat against the ceiling. If a vapor barrier is required, face it toward the heated rooms below, not towards the attic. If, after laying insulation to the top of the joists, you still need to add another layer, install the additional batt as shown in Fig. 13-18. Spread batt over all exposed top plates; plug up all holes; insulate the back of the attic door. *But* don't block any vents.

And now caveats for the loose-fill method: (1) Don't forget to consider the vapor barrier; (2) don't clog any air vents; and (3) don't cover any light fixtures that protrude into the attic floor from below. Beyond these precautions, installing loose fill is just a matter of pouring it in and raking it level.

Glossary

air-dried lumber. Lumber that has been piled in yards or sheds for any length of time. For the United States as a whole, the minimum moisture content of thoroughly air-dired lumber is 12 to 15 percent and the average is somewhat higher. In the South, air-dried lumber may be no lower than 19 percent.

airway. A space between roof insulation and roof boards for movement of air.

alligatoring. Coarse checking pattern characterized by a slipping of the new paint coating over the old coating to the extent that the old coating can be seen through the fissures.

anchor bolts. Bolts to secure a wooden sill plate to concrete or masonry floor or wall.

annular-ring nail. A nail with grooved shank to increase its holding power.

apron. The flat member of the inside trim of a window placed against the wall immediately beneath the stool.

areaway. An open subsurface space adjacent to a building used to admit light or air or as a means of access to a basement.

asphalt. Most native asphalt is a residue from evaporated petroleum. It is insoluble in water but soluble in gasoline and melts when heated. Used widely in building for such items as waterproof roof coverings of many types, exterior wall coverings, and flooring tile.

astragal. A molding, attached to one of a pair of swinging doors, against which the other door strikes.

attic ventilators. In houses, screened openings provided to ventilate an attic space. They are located in the soffit area as inlet ventilators and in the gable end or along the ridge as outlet ventilators. They can also consist of powerdriven fans used as an exhaust system.

—B—

backfill. The replacement of excavated earth into a trench or pier excavation around and against a basement foundation.

balloon framing. A method of construction in which the wall studs extend in one piece from the foundation to the roof.

balustrade. A railing made up of balusters, top rail, and sometimes bottom rail, used on the edge of stairs, balconies, and porches.

balusters. Usually small vertical members in a railing used between a top rail and the stair treads or a bottom rail.

barge board. A decorative board covering the projecting rafter (fly rafter) of the gable end. At the cornice, this member is a facia board.

base molding. Molding used to trim the upper edge of interior baseboard.

base or baseboard. A board placed around a room against the wall next to the floor to finish properly between floor and plaster or dry wall.

base shoe. Molding used next to the floor on interior baseboard. Sometimes called a carpet strip.

batten. Narrow strips of wood used to cover joints or as decorative vertical members over plywood or wide boards.

batter board. One of a pair of horizontal boards nailed to posts set at the corners of an excavation, used to indicate the desired level, also as a fastening for stretched strings to indicate outlines of foundation walls.

batt insulation. Fibrous insulation material fabricated in rectangular form from 15″ to 23″ wide and from 24″ to 48″ long.

bay window. Any window space projecting outward from the walls of a building, either square or polygonal in plan.

beam. A structural member transversely supporting a load.

bearing partition. A partition that supports any vertical load in addition to its own weight.

bearing wall. A wall that supports any vertical load in addition to its own weight.

bed molding. A molding in an angle, as between the overhanging cornice, or eaves, of a building and the sidewalls.

blanket insulation. A fibrous insulating material made in roll form.

blind-nailing. Nailing in such a way that the nailheads are not visible on the face of the work. Usually at the tongue of matched boards.

blind stop. A rectangular molding, usually 3/4 by 1 3/8 inches or more in width, used in the assembly of a window frame. Serves as a stop for storm and screen or combination windows and to resist air infiltration.

block flooring. Flooring in square shapes, usually 9″ × 9″ and made with glued or laminated blocks; edges are tongue-and-groove or grooved all around.

bolts anchor. Bolts to secure a wooden sill plate to concrete or masonry floor or wall or pier.

border tiles. Tiles used at the edges of a room; usually they must be cut to fit.

brace. An inclined piece of framing lumber applied to wall or floor to stiffen the structure. Often used on walls as temporary bracing until framing has been completed.

brick veneer. A facing of brick laid against and fastened to sheathing of a frame wall or tile wall construction.

bridging. Small wood or metal members that are inserted in a diagonal position between the floor joists at midspan to act both as tension and compression members for the purpose of bracing the joists and spreading the action of loads.

British thermal unit (BTU). Symbol representing the amount of heat needed to raise the temperature of 1 pound of water one-degree Fahrenheit.

buck. Often used in reference to rough frame opening hembers. Door bucks used in reference to metal door frame.

—C—

C. Symbol representing the conductance value of a material, showing the amount of heat (BTUs) that will flow through one square foot of material in one hour with a one-degree difference between both its surfaces.

casing. Molding of various widths and thicknesses used to trim door and window openings at the jambs.

casing nail. A nail similar to a finishing nail but with a conical head.

cement blocks. Also called concrete blocks; made of cement, sand crushed rock and gravel in graduated fragments.

cement-coated nail. A rosin coating applied to nails to increase their holding power.

cinder blocks. Similar to cement blocks, but made with volcanic ash instead of crushed rock and lighter in weight.

collar beam. Nominal 1- or 2-inch-thick members connecting opposite roof rafters. They serve to stiffen the roof structure.

column. In architecture: A perpendicular supporting member, circular or rectangular in section, usually consisting of a base, shaft, and capital. In engineering: A vertical structural compression member which supports loads acting in the direction of its longitudinal axis.

combination doors or windows. Combination doors or windows used over regular openings. They provide winter insulation and summer protection. They often have self-storing or removable glass and screen inserts. This eliminates the need for handling a different unit each season.

concrete, plain. Concrete without reinforcement, or reinforced only for shrinkage or temperature changes.

condensation. Beads or drops of water, and frequently frost in extremely cold weather, that accumulate on the inside of the exterior covering of a building when warm, moisture-laden air from the interior reaches a point where the temperature no longer permits the air to sustain the moisture it holds. Use of louvers or attic ventilators will reduce moisture condensation in attics. A vapor barrier under the gypsum lath or drywall on exposed walls will reduce condensation in walls.

construction, drywall. A type of construction in which the interior wall finish is applied in a dry condition, generally in the form of sheet materials or wood paneling, as contrasted to plaster.

construction, frame. A type of construction in which the structural parts are of wood or depend upon a wood frame for support. In building codes, if masonry veneer is applied to the exterior walls, the classification of this type of construction is usually unchanged.

coped joint. Fitting woodwork to an irregular surface. In moldings, cutting the end of one piece to fit the molded face of the other at an interior angle to replace a miter joint.

corner bead. A strip of formed sheet metal, sometimes combined with a strip of metal lath, placed on corners before plastering to reinforce them. Also, a strip of wood finish three-quarters round or angular placed over a plastered corner for protection.

crawl space. A shallow space below the living quarters of a basementless house, sometimes enclosed.

cross-bridging. Diagonal bracing between adjacent floor joists, placed near the center of the joist span to prevent joists from twisting.

crown molding. A molding used on cornice or wherever an interior angle is to be covered.

—D—

dado. A rectangular groove across the width of a board or plank. In interior decoration, a special type of wall treatment.

decay. Disintegration of wood or other substance through the action of fungi.

deck paint. An enamel with a high degree of resistance to mechanical wear, designed for use on such surfaces as porch floors.

density. The mass of substance in a unit volume. When expressed in the metric system (in g per cc), it is numerically equal to the specific gravity of the same substance.

dewpoint. Temperature at which a vapor begins to deposit as a liquid. Applies especially to water in the atmosphere.

direct nailing. To nail perpendicular to the initial surface or to the junction of the pieces joined. Also termed face nailing.

drain tiles. Cylindrical tiles, usually perforated, are used at the base of foundations to carry away ground water.

dressed and matched (tongued and grooved). Boards or planks machined in such a manner that there is a groove on one edge and a correspoonding tongue on the other.

drywall. Interior covering material, such as gypsum board or plywood, which is applied in large sheets or panels.

ducts. In a house, usually round or rectangular metal pipes for distributing warm air from the heating plant to rooms, or air from a conditioning device, or as cold air returns. Ducts are also made of asbestos and composition materials.

—E—

eaves. The overhang of a roof projecting over the walls.

edge-grain. The grain produced when softwood is cut so that the annular rings form an angle greater than 45 degrees with the surface of the board.

end matched. Boards with tongue-and-groove joints at the ends as well as the sides.

end wall. The short wall of a structure.

expansion strip. In flooring, a cork or other resilient strip placed at the edge of flooring to permit expansion.

—F—

face nailing. To nail perpendicular to the initial surface or to the junction of the pieces joined.

facia or fascia. A flat board, band, or face, used sometimes by itself but usually in combination with moldings, often located at the outer face of the cornice.

filler (wood). A heavily pigmented preparation used for filling and leveling off the pores in open-pored woods.

fire-resistive. In the absence of a specific ruling by the authority having jurisdiction, applies to materials for construction not combustible in the temperatures of ordinary fires and that will withstand such fires without serious impairment of their usefulness for at least 1 hour.

fire-retardant chemical. A chemical or preparation of chemicals used to reduce flammability or to retard spread of flame.

footing. A masonry section, usually concrete, in a rectangular form wider than the bottom of the foundation wall or pier it supports.

foundation. The supporting portion of a structure below the first-floor construction, or below grade, including the footings.

framing, balloon. A system of framing a building in which all vertical structural elements of the bearing walls and partitions consist of single pieces extending from the top of the foundation sill plate to the roofplate and to which all floor joists are fastened.

framing, platform. A system of framing a building in which floor joists of each story rest on the top plates of the story below or on the foundation sill for the first story and the bearing walls and partitions rest on the subfloor of each story.

frieze. In house construction, a horizontal member connecting the top of the siding with the soffit of the cornice.

frostline. The depth of frost penetration in soil. This depth varies in different parts of the country. Footings should be placed below this depth to prevent movement.

fungi, wood. Microscopic plants that live in damp wood and cause mold. stain, and decay.

fungicide. A chemical that is poisonous to fungi.

furring. Strips of wood or metal applied to a wall or other surface to even it and normally to serve as a fastening base for finish material.

—G—

gable. The triangular vertical end of a building formed by the eaves and ridge of a sloped roof.

girder. A large or principal beam of wood or steel used to support concentrated loads at isolated points along its length.

gloss (paint or enamel). A paint or enamel that contains a relatively low proportion of pigment and dries to a sheen or luster.

grain. The direction, size, arrangement, appearance, or quality of the fibers in wood.

grain, edge (vertical). Edge-grain lumber has been sawed parallel to the pith of the log and approximately at right angles to the growth rings; i.e., the rings form an angle of 45° or more with the surface of the piece.

grounds. Guides used around openings and at the floorline to strike off plaster. They can consist of narrow strip of wood or of wide subjambs at interior doorways. They provide a level plaster line for installation of casing and other trim.

grout. Mortar made of such consistency (by adding water that it will just flow into the joints and cavities of the masonry work and fill them solid.

gusset. A flat wood, plywood, or similar type member used to provide a connection at the intersection of wood members. Most commonly used at joints of wood trusses. They are fastened by nails, screws, bolts, or adhesives.

—H—

hardwood. Wood from a tree which has broad leaves; most are harder than softwoods, but not all.

header. (a) A beam placed perpendicular to joists and to which joists are nailed in framing for chimney, stairway, or other opening. (b) A wood lintel.

hearth. The inner or outer floor of a fireplace, usually made of brick, tile, or stone.

heartwood. The wood extending from the pith to the sapwood, the cells of which no longer participate in the life process of the tree.

hip. The external angle formed by the meeting of two sloping sides of a roof.

hip roof. A roof that rises by inclined planes from all four sides of a building.

—I—

insulation board, rigid. A structural building board made of wood or cane fiber in 1/2- and 25/32-inch thicknesses. It can be obtained in various size sheets, in various densities, and with several treatments.

insulation, thermal. Any material high in resistance to heat transmission that, when placed in the walls, ceilings, or floors of a structure, will reduce the rate of heat flow.

interior finish. Material used to cover the interior framed areas, or materials of walls and ceilings.

—J—

jack rafter. A rafter that spans the distance from the wallplate to a hip, or from a valley to a ridge.

joint. The space between the adjacent surfaces of two members or components joined and held together by nails, glue, cement, mortar, or other means.

joint cement. A powder that is usually mixed with water and used for joint treatment in gypsum-wallboard finish. Often called Spackle.

joist. One of a series of parallel beams, usually 2 inches thick, used to support floor and ceiling loads, and supported in turn by larger beams, girders, or bearing walls.

joist hanger. A metal bracket used to support joists.

—K—

k. Symbol representing thermal conductivity or the amount of heat (BTUs) that passes through one square foot of material one-inch thick in one hour when there is a one-degree difference Fahrenheit between both its surfaces.

kiln-dried lumber. Lumber that has been kiln dried often to a moisture content of 6 to 12 percent. Common varieties of softwood lumber, such as framing lumber are dried to a somewhat higher moisture content.

—L—

lath. A building material of wood, metal, gypsum, or insulating board that is fastened to the frame of a building to act as a plaster base.

ledger strip. A strip of lumber nailed along the bottom of the side of a girder on which joists rest.

light. Space in a window sash for a single pane of glass. Also, a pane of glass.

lintel. A horizontal structural member that supports the load over an opening such as a door or window.

lookout. A short wood bracket or cantilever to support an over-hanging portion of a roof or the like, usually concealed from view.

louver. An opening with a series of horizontal slats so arranged as to permit ventilation but to exclude rain, sunlight, or vision.

lumber. Lumber is the product of the sawmill and planing mill not further manufactured other than by sawing, resawing, and pas-sing length-wise through a standard planing machine, cross cutting to length, and matching.

lumber, board. Yard lumber less than 2 inches thick and 2 or more inches wide.

lumber, dimension. Yard lumber from 2 inches to, but not includ-ing, 5 inches thick, and 2 or more inches wide. Includes joists, rafters, studs, plank, and small timbers. The actual size dimen-sion of such lumber after shrinking from green dimension and after machining to size or pattern is called the dress size.

lumber, matched. Lumber that is dressed and shaped on one edge in a grooved pattern and on the other in a tongued pattern.

lumber, yard. Lumber of those grades, sizes, and patterns which are generally intended for ordinary construction, such as framework and rough coverage of houses.

lumber, timbers. Yard lumber 5 or more inches in least dimension. Includes beams, stringers, posts, caps, sills, girders, and pur-lins.

—M—

masonry. Stone, brick, concrete, hollow-tile, concrete-block, gypsum-block, or other similar building units or mate-rials or a combination of the same, bonded together with mortar to form a wall, pier, buttress, or similar mass.

mastic. A pasty material used as a cement (as for setting tile) or a protective coating (as for thermal insulation or waterproofing).

metal lath. Sheets of metal that are slit and drawn out to form openings. Used as a plaster base for walls and ceilings and as reinforcing over other forms of plaster base.

millwork. Generally all building materials made of finished wood and manufactured in millwork plants and planing mills are included under the term "millwork." It includes such items as inside and outside doors, window and doorframes, blinds, porchwork, mantels, panelwork, stairways, moldings, and interior trim. It normally does not include flooring, ceiling, or siding.

miter joint. The joint of two pieces at an angle that bisects the joining angle. For example, the miter joint at the side and head casing at a door opening is made at a 45° angle.

moisture content of wood. Weight of the water contained in the wood, usually expressed as a percentage of the weight of the ovendry wood.

mortise. A slot cut into a board, plank, or timber, usually edgewise, to receive tenon of another board, plank, or timber to form a joint.

molding. A wood strip having a curved or projecting surface used for decorative purposes.

—N—

nailer. A strip of wood or blocking which serves as a backing into which nails can be driven.

natural finish. A transparent finish which does not seriously alter the original color or grain of the natural wood. Natural finishes are usually provided by sealers, oils, varnishes, water-repellent preservatives, and other similar materials.

nonloadbearing wall. A wall supporting no load other than its own weight.

notch. A crosswise rabbet at the end of a borad.

—O—

O.C. On center. The measurement of spacing for studs, rafters, joists, and the like in a building from the center of one member to the center of the next.

outrigger. An extension of a rafter beyond the wall line. Usually a smaller member nailed to a larger rafter to form a cornice or roof overhang.

—P—

paint. A combination of pigments with suitable thinners or oils to provide decorative and protective coatings.

panel. In house construction, a thin flat piece of wood, plywood, or similar material, framed by stiles and rails as in a door or fitted into grooves of thicker material with molded edges for decorative wall treatment.

paper, sheathing or building. A building material, generally paper or felt, used in wall and roof construciton as a protection against the passage of air and sometimes moisture.

particleboard. A highly compressed panel made of wood chips and resin.

partition. A wall that subdivides spaces within any story of a building.

partition wall. An interior wall separating one area of a house from another.

penny. As applied to nails, it originally indicated the price per hundred. The term now serves as a measure of nail length and is abbreviated by the letter *d*.

perm. A measure of water vapor movement through a material (grains per square foot per hour per inch of mercury difference in vapor pressure).

pier. A column of masonry, usually rectangular in horizontal cross section, used to support other structural members.

pigment. A powdered solid in suitable degree of subdivision for use in paint or enamel.

pilot hole. A preliminary hole drilled in wood to receive a screw or nail.

pitch. The incline slope of a roof, or the ratio of the total rise to the total width of a house; i.e., an 8-foot rise and a 24-foot width are a 1/3 pitch roof. *Roof slope* is expressed in inches of rise per 12 inches of run.

pitch pocket. A cavity in wood containing pitch (resin).

plank flooring. Wood flooring in from 3 1/2

plate. Sill plate: a horizontal member anchored to a masonry wall. Sole plate: bottom horizontal member of a frame wall. Top plate: top horizontal member of a frame wall supporting ceiling joists, rafters, or other members.

platform framing. A method of construction in which each floor is framed independently; the joists of the floor above rest on the top plate of the floor below.

plaster ground. A strip of wood used as a thickness gauge when plastering a wall; usually placed at the floor and around windows and doors.

plug. A piece used to fill a hole.

plumb. Exactly perpendicular; vertical.

plywood. A piece of wood made of three or more layers of veneer joined with glue and usually laid with the grain of adjoining plies at right angles. Almost always an odd number of plies are used to provide balanced construction.

preservative. Any substance that, for a reasonable length of time, will prevent the action of wood-destroying fungi, borers of various kinds, and similar destructive life when the wood has been properly coated or impregnated with it.

pressure-sensitive. An adhesive backing which sticks upon contact when slight pressure is applied.

primer. The first coat of paint in a paint job that consists of two or more coats; also the paint used for such a first coat.

putty. A type of cement usually made of whiting and boiled linseed oil, beaten or kneaded to the consistency of dough, and used in sealing glass in sash, filling small holes and crevices in wood, and for similar purposes.

—Q—

quarter round. A small molding that has the cross section of a quarter circle.

quarter-sawed. Hardwood cut so that annular rings form an angle greater than 45 degrees with the face of the board.

—R—

R. Symbol representing the measured resistance of a material to the flow of heat.

rabbet. A rectangular longitudinal groove cut in the corner edge of a board or plank.

radiant heating. A method of heating, usually consisting of a forced hot water system with pipes placed in the floor, wall, or ceiling; or with electrically heated panels.

radiation. The transfer of heat by electromagnetic waves from a warmer to a cooler body.

rafter. One of a series of structural members of a roof designed to support roof loads. The rafters of a flat roof are sometimes called roof joists.

rafter, hip. A rafter that forms the intersection of an external roof angle.

rafter, valley. A rafter that forms the intersection of an internal roof angle. The valley rafter is normally made of doubled 2-inch-thick members.

rail. Cross members of panel doors or of a sash. Also the upper and lower members of a balustrade or staircase extending from one vertical support, such as a post, to another.

rake. The inclined edge of a gable roof (the trim member is a rake molding).

reflective insulation. An insulating material consisting of highly reflective surfaces.

resilient flooring. Any vinyl- or asphalt-base floor covering with a certain amount of resistance to denting or deformation; usually installed over plywood subflooring and underlayment.

ribbon. A horizontal timber nailed to the face of the studs; it usually supports floor joists.

ridge. The horizontal line at the junction of the top edges of two sloping roof surfaces.

ridge board. The board placed on edge at the ridge of the roof into which the upper ends of the rafters are fastened.

roll roofing. Roofing material, composed of fiber and saturated with asphalt, that is supplied in rolls containing 108 square feet in 36-inch widths. It is generally furnished in weights of 45 to 90 pounds per roll.

roof sheathing. The boards or sheet material fastened to the roof rafters on which the shingle or other roof covering is laid.

rough opening. The opening in a framed structure.

—S—

sash. A single light frame containing one or more lights of glass.

saturated felt. A felt which is impregnated with tar or asphalt.

sealer. A finishing material, either clear or pigmented, that is usually applied directly over uncoated wood for the purpose of sealing the surface.

sealer strip. The layer of material, usually fiberglass, placed between the sill and top of the foundation wall; it keeps out drafts and insects.

semigloss paint or enamel. A paint or enamel made with a slight insufficiency of nonvolatile vehicle so that its coating, when dry, has some luster but is not very glossy.

shake. A thick handsplit shingle, resawed to form two shakes; usually edge grained.

sheathing. The structural covering, usually wood boards or plywood, used over studs or rafters of a structure. Structural building board is normally used only as wall sheathing.

shellac. A transparent coating made by dissolving lac, a resinous secretion of the lac bug (a scale insect that thrives in tropical countries, especially India), in alcohol.

shingles. Roof covering of asphalt, asbestos, wood, tile, slate, or other material cut to stock lengths, widths, and thicknesses.

side walls. The long walls of a structure.

sill. The lowest ember of the frame of a structure, resting on the foundation and supporting the floor joists or the uprights of the wall. The member forming the lower side of an opening, as a door sill, window sill, etc.

sill anchor. A fastener projecting from a foundation wall or slab and used for securing the sill.

slab. A concrete floor poured on a prepared ground site.

sleeper. Usually, a wood member embedded in concrete, as in a floor, that serves to support and to fasten subfloor or flooring.

soffit. Usually the underside covering of an overhangng cornice.

softwood. Wood from a tree with needle-like leaves and cones such as pine or spruce; all evergreens are softwood trees.

soil cover (ground cover). A light covering of plastic film, roll roofing, or similar material used over the soil in crawl spaces of buildings to minimize moisture permeation of the area.

sole plate. The bottom horizontal member of a wall.

solid bridging. A solid member placed between adjacent floor joists near the center of the span to prevent joists from twisting.

span. The distance between structural supports such as walls, columns, piers, beams, girders, and trusses.

square. A unit of measure—100 square feet—usually applied to roofing material. Sidewall coverings are sometimes packed to cover 100 square feet and are sold on that basis.

strip flooring. Wood flooring consisting of narrow, matched strips.

string, stringer. A timber or other support for cross members in floors or ceilings. In stairs, the support on which the stair treads rest; also stringboard.

stud. One of a series of slender wood or metal vertical structural members placed as supporting elements in walls and partitions. (Plural: studs or studding).

subfloor. Boards or plywood laid on joists over which a finish floor is to be laid.

—T—

tail beam. A relatively short beam or joist supported in a wall on one end and by a header at the other.

termites. Insects that superficially resemble ants in size, general appearance, and habit of living in colonies; hence, frequently called "white ants." Subterranean termites *do not* establish themselves in buildings by being carried in with lumber, but by entering from ground nests after the building has been constructed. If unmolested, they eat out the woodwork, leaving a shell of sound wood to conceal their activities, and damage may proceed so far so to cause collapse of parts of a structure before discovery. There are about 56 species of termites known in the United States; but the two main species, classified from the manner in which they attack wood, subterranean (ground-inhabiting) termites, the most common, and dry-wood termites, are found almost exclusively along the extreme southern border and the Gulf of Mexico in the United States.

termite shield. A shield, usually of noncorrodible metal, placed in or on a foundation wall or other mass of masonry or around pipes to prevent passage of termites.

threshold. A strip of wood or metal with beveled edges used over the finished floor and the sill of exterior doors.

toenailing. To drive a nail at a slant with the initial surface in order to permit it to penetrate into a second member.

tongue and groove. Shapes cut into the edge of boards. The tongue is a projection which fits into the groove or rectangular channel of the mating piece.

trim. The finish materials in a building, such as moldings, applied around openings (window trims, door trim) or at the floor and ceiling of rooms (baseboard, cornice, picture molding).

trimmer. A beam or joist to which a header is nailed in framing for a chimney, stairway, or other opening.

truss. A frame or jointed structure designed to act as a beam of long span, while each member is usually subjected to longitudinal stress only, either tension or compression.

—U—

U. Symbol representing the heat loss through a building section in BTU's per hour.

undercoat. A coating applied prior to the finishing or top coats of a paint job. It may be the first of two or the second of three coats. In some usage of the word, it may become synonymous with priming coat.

underlayment. A material placed under finish coverings such as flooring, or shingles, to provide a smooth, even surface for applying the finish.

—V—

vapor barrier. A material used to retard the movement of water vapor into or through walls, floors, and ceilings.

varnish. A thickened preparation of drying oil or drying oil and resin suitable for spreading on surfaces to form continuous, transparent coatings, or for mixing with pigments to make enamels.

vermiculite. Particles of a lightweight mineral with insulating qualities, used as bulk insulation.

vinyl. A tough, durable plastic.

—W—

water-repellent preservative. A liquid designed to penetrate into wood and impart water repellency and a moderate preservative protection. It is used for millwork, such as sash and frames, and is usually applied by dipping.

weatherstrip. Narrow or jamb-width sections of thin metal or other material to prevent infiltration of air and moisture around windows and doors.

Appendices

Appendix A
Ceiling Framing

CEILING JOISTS

After exterior and interior walls are plumbed, braced, and top plates added, ceiling joists can be positioned and nailed in place. They are normally placed across the width of the house, as are the rafters. The parititions of the house are usually located so that ceiling joists of even lengths (10, 12, 14, and 16 ft. or longer) can be used without waste to span from exterior walls to load-bearing interior walls. The sizes of the joists depend on the span, wood species, spacing between joists, and the load on the second floor or attic. The correct sizes for various conditions can be found in joist tables or designated local building requirements. When preassembled trussed rafters (roof trusses) are used, the lower chord acts as the ceiling joist. The truss also eliminates the need for load-bearing partitions.

Second grades of the various species are commonly used for ceiling joists and rafters. It is also desirable, particularly in two-story houses and when material is available, to limit the moisture content of the second-floor joists to no more than 15 percent. This applies as well to other lumber used throughout the house. Maximum moisture content for dimension material should be 19 percent.

Ceiling joists are used to support ceiling finishes. They often act as floor joists for second and attic floors and as ties between exterior walls and interior partitions. Since ceiling joists also serve as tension members to resist the thrust of the rafters of pitched roofs, they

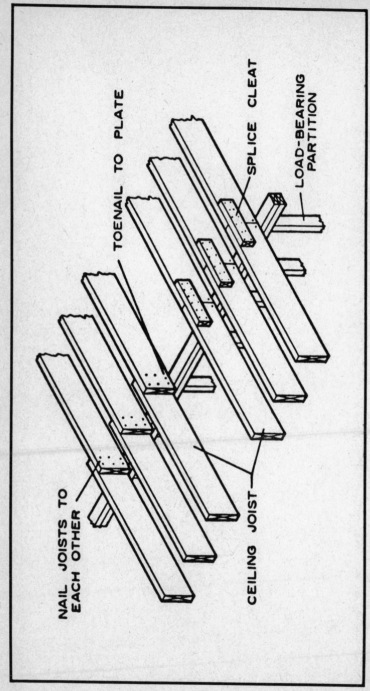

Fig. A-1. A typical ceiling joist configuration.

204

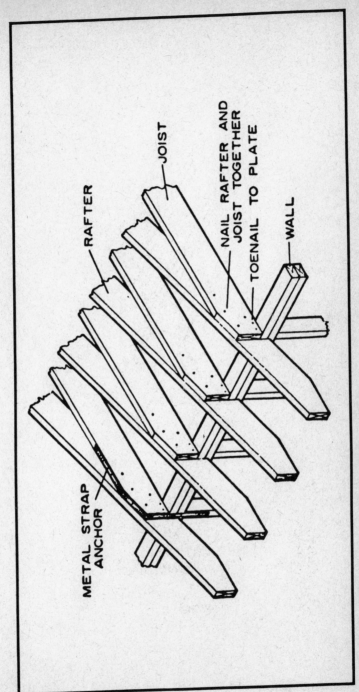

JOIST

RAFTER

NAIL RAFTER AND
JOIST TOGETHER

TOENAIL TO PLATE

WALL

METAL STRAP
ANCHOR

Fig. A-2. Ceiling joists are nailed to the rafters and top plates.

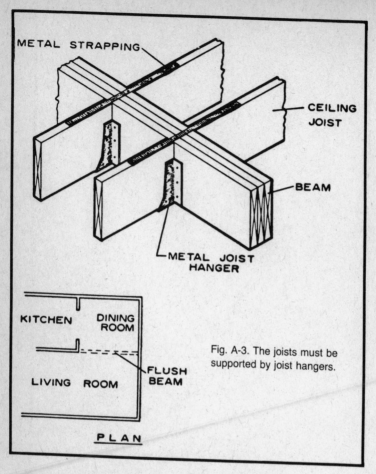

METAL STRAPPING

CEILING JOIST

BEAM

METAL JOIST HANGER

KITCHEN

DINING ROOM

LIVING ROOM

FLUSH BEAM

PLAN

Fig. A-3. The joists must be supported by joist hangers.

must be securely nailed to the plate at outer and inner walls. They are also nailed together, directly or with wood or metal cleats, where they cross or join at the load-bearing partition (Fig. A-1) and to the rafter at the exterior walls (Fig. A-2). Toenail at each wall.

In areas of severe windstorms, the use of metal strapping or other systems of anchoring ceiling and roof framing to the wall is good practice. When ceiling joists are perpendicular to rafters, collar beams and cross ties should be used to resist thrust. The in-line joist system can also be adapted to ceiling or second floor joists.

FLUSH CEILING FRAMING

In many house designs, the living room and the dining or family room from an open "L." A wide, continuous ceiling area between the

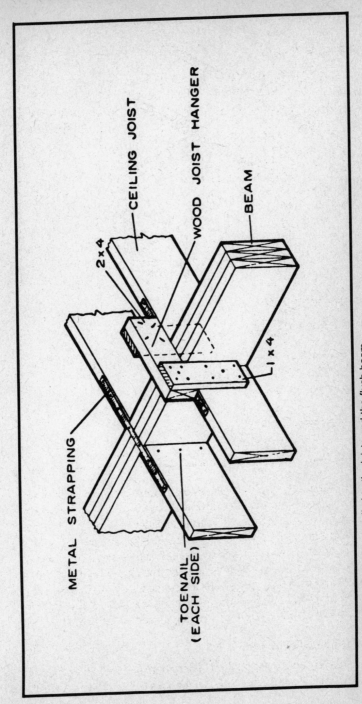

CEILING JOIST

WOOD JOIST HANGER

BEAM

2 x 4

1 x 4

METAL STRAPPING

TOENAIL
(EACH SIDE)

Fig. A-4. Wood joist hangers are nailed to the joists and the flush beam.

207

two rooms is often desirable. This can be created with a flush beam, which replaces the load-bearing partitions used in the remainder of the house. A nail-laminated beam, designed to carry the ceiling load, supports the ends of the joists. Joists are toenailed into the beam and supported by metal joist hangers (Fig. A-3) or wood hangers (Fig. A-4). To resist the thrust of the rafters for longer spans, it is often desirable to provide added resistance by using metal strapping. Strapping should be nailed to each opposite joist with three or four eightpenny nails.

Appendix B
Joists for Different
Floor Systems

The size and lengths of floor joists, as well as the species and spacing, are usually shown in the floor framing layout in the working plans for the house being built. The joists may vary from nominal 2 by 8 inches in size to 2 by 10 inches or larger where spans are long. Moisture content of floor joists and other floor framing members should not exceed 19 percent when possible. Spacing of joists is normally 16 or 24 inches on center so that 8-foot lengths of plywood for subfloor will span six or four joist spaces.

In low-cost houses, savings can be made by using plywood for subfloor which also serves as a base for resilient tile or other covering. This can be done by specifying tongued-and-grooved edges in a plywood grade of C-C plugged Exterior Douglar-fir, southern pine, or similar species. Regular Interior Underlayment grade with exterior glue is also considered satisfactory. The *matched* edges provide a tight lengthwise joint, and end joints are made over the joists. If tongued-and-grooved plywood is not available, use square edged plywood and block between joists with 2 by 4's for edge nailing. Plywood subfloor also serves as a tie between joists over the center beam.

Single-floor systems can also include the use of nominal 1- by 4-inch matched finish flooring in species such as southern pine and Douglas-fir and the lower grades of oak, birch, and maple in 25/32-inch thickness. To prevent air and dust infiltration, joists should first be covered with 15-pound asphalt felt or similar materials. The flooring is then applied over the floor joists and the flood insulation added when the house is enclosed. When this single-floor system is used, however, some surface protection from weather and mechanical damage is required. A full-width sheet of heavy plastic or similar covering can be used, and the walls erected directly over the film. When most of the exterior and interior work is done, the covering can be removed and the floor sanded and finished.

POST FOUNDATION—WITH SIDE OVERHANG

The joists for a low-cost house are usually the third grade of such species as southern pine or Douglas-fir and are often 2 by 8 inches in size for spans of approximately 12 feet. If an overhang of about 12 inches is used for 12-foot lengths, the joist spacing normally can be 24 inches. Sizes, spacing, and other details are shown in the plans for each individual house.

The joists can now be cut to length, using a *butt joint* over the center beam. Thus, for a 24-foot-wide house, each pair of joists should be cut to a 12-foot length, less the thickness of the end header joist which is usually 1½ inches. The edge or stringer joists should be positioned on the beams with several other joists and the premarked headers nailed to them with one sixteen penny nail (or just enough to keep them in postiion). The frame, including the edge (stringer) joists and the header joists, is now the exact outline of the house. Square up this framework by using the equal diagonal method. The overhang beyond the beams should be the same at each side of the house. Now, with eightpenny nails, *toenail* the joists to each beam they cross and the stringer joists to the beam beneath (Fig. 3-1) to hold the framwork exactly square. Add the remaining joists and nail the headers into the ends with three sixteen penny nails. Toenail the remaining joists to the headers with eightpenny nails. When the center of a parallel partition wall is more than 4 inches from the center of the joists, add solid blocking between the joists. The blocking should be the same size as the joists and spaced not more than 3 feet apart. Toenail blocking to the joists with two tenpenny nails at each side.

In moderate climates, 1-inch blanket insulation may be sufficient to insulate the floor of crawl-space houses. It is usually placed between the joists in the same way that thicker insulation is normally installed. Another method consists of rolling 24-inch-wide 1-inch insulation across the joists, nailing or stapling it where necessary to keep it stretched with tight edge joints (Fig. B-1). Insulation of this type should have strong damage-resistant covers. Tenpenny ring-shank nails should be used to fasten the plywood to the joists rather

210

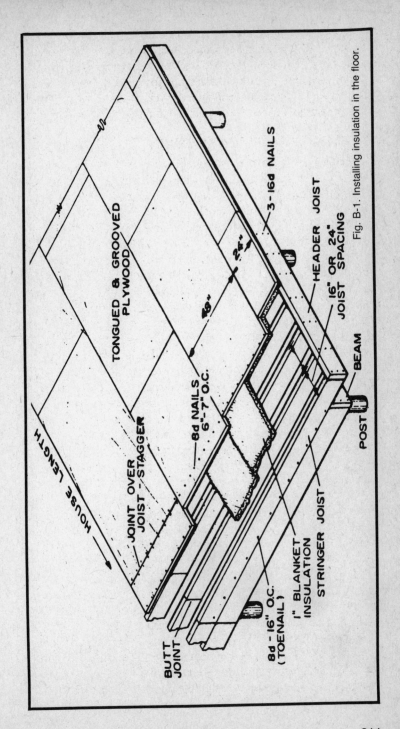

Fig. B-1. Installing insulation in the floor.

HOUSE LENGTH

TONGUED & GROOVED PLYWOOD

JOINT OVER JOIST - STAGGER

8d NAILS 6-7" O.C.

3-16d NAILS

HEADER JOIST

16" OR 24" JOIST SPACING

BEAM

POST

STRINGER JOIST

1" BLANKET INSULATION

8d - 16" O.C. (TOENAIL)

BUTT JOINT

211

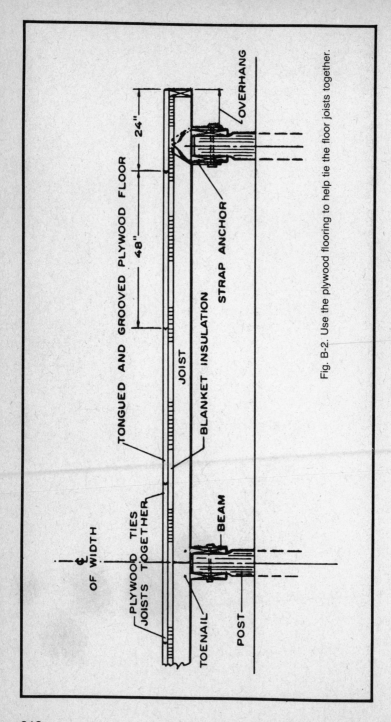

Fig. B-2. Use the plywood flooring to help tie the floor joists together.

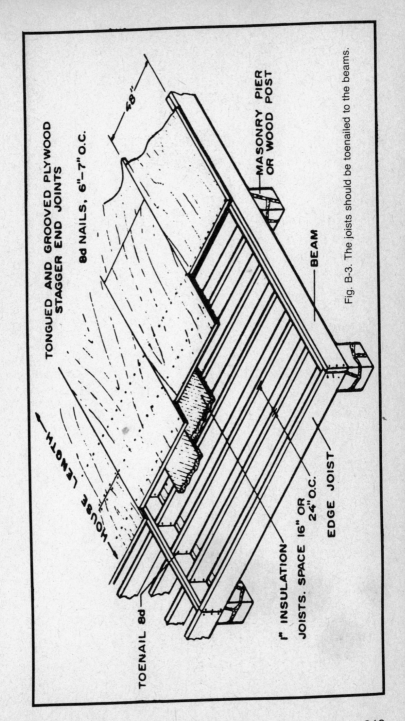

TONGUED AND GROOVED PLYWOOD
STAGGER END JOINTS

8d NAILS, 6"–7" O.C.

48"

HOUSE LENGTH

TOENAIL 8d

1" INSULATION. SPACE 16" OR
JOISTS. SPACE 16" OR 24" O.C.

EDGE JOIST

MASONRY PIER
OR WOOD POST

BEAM

Fig. B-3. The joists should be toenailed to the beams.

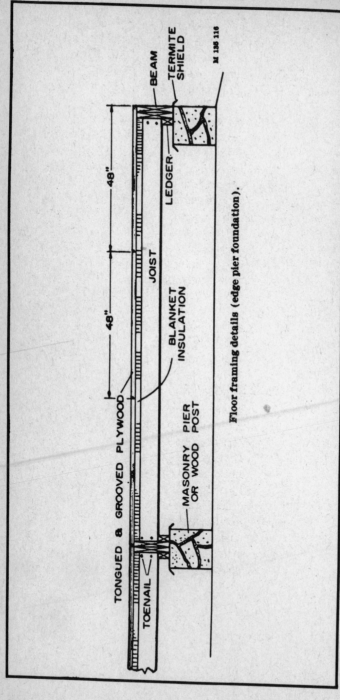

TONGUED & GROOVED PLYWOOD

TOENAIL

48"

48"

BEAM

TERMITE SHIELD

LEDGER

JOIST

BLANKET INSULATION

MASONRY OR WOOD POST

M 135 116

Floor framing details (edge pier foundation).

Fig. B-4. Use 4-foot-wide plywood sheets for the subflooring.

than eightpenny common normally used. This will minimize nail movement or "nail pops" which could occur during moisture changes. The vapor barrier of the insulation should be on the upper side toward the subfloor. Two-inch and thicker blanket or batt insulation is placed between the joists and should be applied any time after the floor is in place, preferably when the house is near completion.

When the house is 20, 24, 28, or 32 feet wide, the first row of tongued-and-grooved plywood sheets should be 24 inches wide, so that the butt-joints of the joists at the center beam are reinforced with a full 48-inch-wide piece (Fig. B-2). This plywood is usually ⅝- or ¾-inch thick when it serves both as subfloor and underlayment. Rip 4-foot-wide pieces in half and save the other halves for the opposite side. Place the square, sawed edges flush with the header and nail the plywood to each crossing joist and header with eightpenny common nails spaced 6 to 7 inches apart at edges and at intermediate joists (Fig. B-1). Joints in the next full 4-foot widths of plywood should be broken by starting at one end with a 4-foot long piece. End joints will thus be staggered 48 inches. End joints should always be staggered 48 inches. End joints should always be staggered at least one joist space, 16 or 24 inches. Be sure to draw up the tongued-and-grooved edges tightly. A chalked snap-string should be used to mark the position of the joists for nailing.

EDGE FOUNDATION-MASONRY PIER OR WOOD POST

When edge piers or wood posts are used with edge support beams, the joists can be cut to length to fit snugly between the center and outside beams so that they rest on the ledger strips. Sizes of headers, joists, and other details are usually shown on the working drawings for each individual house. Toenail each end to the beams with two eightpenny nails on each side (Fig. B-3). In applying the plywood subfloor to the floor framing, start with full 4-foot-wide sheets rather than the 2-foot-wide pieces used for the side overhang framing (Fig. B-4). The nail-laminated center beam provides sufficient reinforcing between the ends of joists. Apply the insulation and nail the plywood the same way as outlined in the previous section.

Appendix C
Characteristics
of Flooring Materials

SUBFLOORS

Usual requirements:

Lumber—Requirements are not exacting, but moderate stiffness, medium shrinkage and warp, and ease of working are desired.

Plywood—Moderate stiffness when finish in strip flooring; high stiffness for wood block or resilient finish flooring. Good nail-holding qualities.

Softwood plywoods for use as subfloors with or without underlayment are classified by density, hence stiffness and strength, into groups. For each grouping a limit for span and loading is established. This is shown on each piece of plywood by a number such as "32/16." The first number indicates maximum span when used as roof sheathing and the second number indicates maximum span when used as subfloor. Here "16" indicates that the maximum span for living area space is framing 16 inches on centers.

Woods combining usual requirements in a *high* degree:

Lumber—Douglas-fir, western larch, and southern yellow pine. (Commonly used.)

Ash and oak. (Seldom used because of adaptability to more exacting uses.)

Plywood—Group 1 and 2 softwoods such as: Douglas-fir, southern yellow pine, and western larch.

Woods combining usual requirements in a *good* degree:

Lumber—Hemlock, ponderosa pine, spruce, lodgepole pine, aspen, balsam fir, and white fir. (Commonly used.)

Northern and Idaho white pine, sugar pine, and poplar. (Seldom used because of adaptability to more exacting uses.)

Beech, birch, elm, hackberry, maple, oak, and tupelo. (Not used extensively, harder to work. Maple, elm, and oak often available locally.)

Plywood—Group 3 and 4 softwoods such as: Cedar, redwood, Sitka and Englemann spruce, west coast hemlock, noble fir, and white fir.

Grades and types used (minimum recommended):

Lumber—Third grade softwood boards are used extensively in better quality houses. In lower cost houses, both third ane fourth grades are used. The fourth garde is serviceable and does not entail much waste, but is not as tight as the higher grades. When hardwoods are used, second grade boards are commonly used in the more expensive houses and third grade in the lower cost houses.

Plywood—Standard interior grade (C-D) under ordinary conditions; in baths, kitchens, or when exposed to weather use Standard grade with exterior glue.

UNDERLAYMENT FOR FINISH FLOORS

Ordinarily all finish flooring except standard strip flooring and 1/2- or 3/4-inch wood block floor, is laid with an underlayment between the subfloor and the finish flooring. This is especially necessary for resilient floor surfacing (rubber, vinyl, vinyl asbestos, or asphalt in tile or sheet form) because of its thinness, flexibility, and tendency to "showthrough" the pattern of the surface beneath it.

Floor underlayment serves the following functions:

1. Provides uniform support for finish flooring.
2. Bridges small irregularities in the subsurface.
3. Because joints in floor underlayment do not coincide with those in subfloor, there is less chance for working of joints to loosen or break finish flooring.
4. Provides a smooth, uncontaminated surface for gluing to the base those kinds of finish flooring requiring it.
5. Permits vertical adjustment in floor levels so all rooms are at the same elevation even when different floorings are used. The subfloor usually serves as the working platform. During the period between initial laying of subfloor and installation of finish flooring the surface may be roughened from wetting, dented from impacts, or contaminated with plaster, dirt, grease, and paint, in fact anything that is tracked or brought into the building.

Some use of combined subfloor-underlayment is developing, particularly in factory-built or tract-built housing where subfloors are given special protection during construction or where pad and carpet are installed.

Floor underlayments are plywood, hardboard, or particleboard.

Plywood underlayment—Plywood underlayment is a special grade produced for this purpose from group 1 woods (for indentation resistance). It is produced in 1/4-, 3/8-, 1/2-, 5/8-, and 3/4-inch thickness, and the face ply is C plugged grade (no voids) with a special C or better veneer underlying the face ply to prevent penetration from such concentrated loads as high heels.

Particleboard underlayment—Produced in the same thicknesses as plywood, particleboard underlayment is often preferred because its uniform surface and somewhat higher density make it more resistant to indentation than plywood when thin resilient flooring is applied over it. Because it tends to change more in length and width with changes in moisture content than plywood, manufacturers' directions for installation and specifications for adhesives must be followed for good performance.

Hardboard underlayment—Produced in 4-foot squares, 0.220 inch thick and planed to uniform thickness, hardboard underlayment should be installed to manufacturers' specifications for proper performance. It is mainly used on remodeling or in new construction where minimum thickness buildup is desired.

STRIP AND WOOD BLOCK

Usual requirements: High resistance to wear, attractive figure or color, minimum warp and shrinkage. (Material should be used at a moisture content near the level it will average in service.)

Woods combining usual requirements in a *high* degree: Maple, red and white oak, beech, and birch. (Most commonly used hardwoods.)

White ash and walnut. (Not commonly used.)

Hickory and pecan. (Not commonly available. Harder to work and nail. More suitable to woodblock flooring.)

Woods combining usual requirements in a *good* degree: Cherry, gum, and sycamore (edge grain). (Not commonly available. Highly decorative and suitable where wear is not severe.)

Cypress, Douglas-fir, west coast hemlock, western larch, and southern yellow pine (edge grain). More suitable in low-cost houses in bedrooms where traffic is light.)

Grades used: In beech, birch, and maple flooring the grade of Firsts is ordinarily used for better quality homes, and Seconds and sometimes Thirds in ecomony houses. In oak, the grade of Clear (either flat or edge grain) is used in better construction, and Selects and sometimes No. 1 Common in lower cost work or where small tight knots provide the desired effect. Other hardwoods are ordinarily used in the same grades as oak.

When softwood flooring is used (without covering) in better quality homes, grade A or B and Better edge grain is used. Grade D or C (edge grain) is used in low-cost homes.

Index

Index